# FISHING GUIDE to the UPPER KEYS & FLORIDA BAY

## Key Largo to Upper Marathon
## Florida Bay & Flamingo

By
**Martin Smithson**

# Fishing Guide To The Upper Keys and Florida Bay
Key Largo to Upper Marathon - Florida Bay and Flamingo

By Martin S. Smithson


∞ ∞ ∞ ∞

Published by:
Fishsonian Publications
P.O. Box 878
Melbourne, Florida  32902


Publication layout and design by:
Cape Canaveral Scientific, Inc., Melbourne Beach, FL.

∞ ∞ ∞ ∞

Library of Congress Catalog Card Number:  97-90900
ISBN  0-9640779-2-2

∞ ∞ ∞ ∞


## DISCLAIMER
No statement made in this book and no reference to any product or procedure shall create any warranty or guarantee that the product or procedure is fit for any particular purpose. Statements or descriptions are for informational purposes only and are not made nor given as a warranty or guarantee and should not be relied on by the reader without independent investigation. All maps and aerial photographs in this book are for general reference only and not intended to be used for navigation. The publisher assumes no responsibility for the accuracy of this information. It is recommended that NOAA and USCG navigation charts be used.

# Contents

## All About

## Aerial Photo Section (Aerials #1 through #24)

# Preface

This book was created to be used as a tool to help the Keys angler successfully explore new areas, find fish in a variety of situations, and to gain an appreciation for the wonderful, diverse, yet sensitive aquatic resources of the Keys and Florida Bay.

If you read "nothing else but" in this book, please read the two chapters titled "Easy on the Grass Flats" and "Fishing Etiquette & Ethics." One inevitable fact of Florida is that the number of residents, visitors and anglers is going to grow exponentially over the next 15 years. Our approach to stalking the fish, protecting their homes and fishing amongst one another will have to change in order to sustain the pleasure of angling. It is my hope, along with many others, that everyone will practice catch and release and work harder towards individually being a plus factor in preserving the fishing for Florida's future.

## About the Author

Martin Smithson's enthusiasm for Florida and fishing is inherited from his dad who was born and raised on the Halifax River in Daytona Beach. As a boy, Marty well remembers the adventuresome fish stories his dad would tell about wading the flats with a gig and using hand lines from the pier. The Smithson family moved to Tennessee but returned to Florida every summer. From the summers of the late 1950's through the 70's Marty watched the Halifax fishery decline.

Marty was schooled at East Tennessee State University where he attended graduate school specializing in fisheries biology. He became an environmental professional in private industry and has worked on some of the largest river and stream restoration projects in the southeast United States. His efforts towards the protection of the Indian River Lagoon have continued for over ten years and led to his publishing the "Indian River Flats Fishing Guide," now a standard reference for fishing the east coast Indian River. Currently he is the Indian River Program Office Director for the St. Johns River Water Management District, and writes a monthly "Marine Environments" column for *Florida Today* newspaper. Marty is an active member in the Florida Sport Fishing Association, Backcountry Fly Fishing Association, Space Coast Sportfishing Foundation and the Florida Outdoor Writers Association.

Marty, his wife LeAnn, and their three children make their home in Melbourne and spend many enjoyable hours on the Indian River and frequenting the Keys.

# Acknowledgements

## This book is dedicated to my family.

∞∞∞∞∞∞∞∞∞∞∞∞∞∞

It is very difficult to think of everyone who contributed in some way to making this book possible. Along the way there have been those who provided inspiration, guidance, advice and other useful pieces of information. It may have been the outdoor writer who provided motivational articles in "Florida Sportsman" or "Fly Fishing in Saltwaters" magazines, a Sunday newspaper, or the many other books on the topic of fishing. Or the conversations with fellow anglers, professional guides, tackle shop owners and other outdoor writers. I am indebted to all of these people and grateful for their contribution to this fine sport.

No book is possible without the expertise of a graphics designer who actually makes it look like a book. A special thanks to Amy W. Adams, managing director of Cape Canaveral Scientific, Inc. at 220 Surf Road in Melbourne Beach, Florida 32951, (407) 722-1161.

Additional thanks to Bonnie Bower-Dennis of Vero Beach, Florida for her complementary illustrations. Also thanks to Diane Rome Peebles of Gulf Coast Graphics in St. Petersburg, Florida for her biological illustrations which appear courtesy of the Florida Marine Research Institute at the Florida Department of Environmental Protection.

**The following people deserve a special thank you:**

LeAnn Smithson—my wife and Editor-In-Chief
Rob Smithson—my son and favorite fishing companion
Captain Hank Brown
Joy Brown
Derek Busby
Scott Deal—Maverick Boat Company
Digital Graphics—Bill Hamilton, Bill Peterson (printing),
Lisa DeMitchell (cover and aerial graphics)
Captain Paul Glanville
Norma Glanville
John Hill
Walter "Bud" Hill
Captain Bob Johnson—Papa Joe's Marina
Brian Lightle
Cdr. John Moore—USN Retired
Steve Morgan
Mark Nichols—D.O.A. Lures
Chuck Padera
Flip Pallot
Captain Don Perchalski
William Potter
Bill Sargent
Gary Walker—Walker & Associates

# About the Cover

## Front Cover
*(Design and photography
by Fishsonian Publications.)*

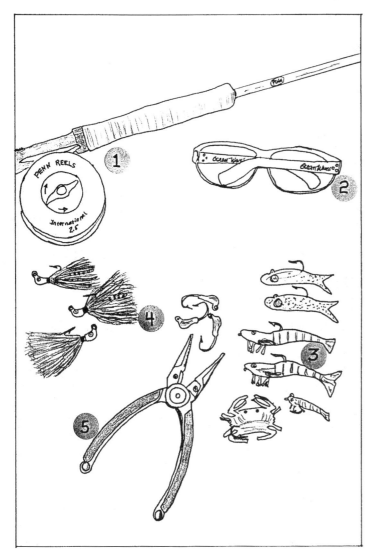

*See following descriptions of numbered products.*
Illustration by Martin Smithson.

The products represented on the front cover are, in my opinion, high quality, reliable performers that will enhance any Florida Keys saltwater fishing experience. These particular items have been proven to consistently work well and are highly respected in the Keys. If I had to put together a Keys angler survival kit, these items would be included.

(1.) Penn® rods and reels have been around a long time and are known for their durability. The Penn International® fly reel pictured is machined from the highest grade marine aluminum and anodized gold for a lifetime of corrosion resistance. This reel contains an oversize drag which assures flawless performance, no matter what fish you pursue. I expect a future generation family member will be using my Penn® reel.

The reel is matched with a Gold Medal® fly rod. The blank is built with 96 percent "IM6" graphite and blended with Penn's exclusive Epoxy resin. Pictured is my nine foot, eight weight rod. Penn® has manufactured fly rods for 35 years. I like the feel of this outfit.

(2.) Ocean Waves® sunglasses are indeed some of the best in the world. If you are going to spend any time in the Florida Keys sun, say over 20 minutes, you need good glasses! Pictured is a Nassau style with backwater green lenses. The optical quality and clarity of these glasses is superior to any I have owned. The combined polarizing film with an anti-reflective coating is sandwiched between two thin glass lenses and seem impossible to scratch. These glasses not only allow you to see everything in the water but also protect your eyes from UV light and eye strain. I won't go out on the boat without them.

(3.) Mark Nichols, founder of D.O.A.® lures,

doesn't package lures to capture fishermen, he perfects his soft baits to catch fish. I have known Mark for several years and have been impressed at how many hours he spends on the water adjusting and perfecting his creations. Mark spent considerable time in the Keys and has come up with an artificial lure that mimics bait that the tarpon can't resist, especially around the bridges and passes. The TerrorEyz® pictured, have actually proved to be more effective on Channel 2 tarpon, jumping more fish than several anglers using live bait. These baits make "eye contact" with their holographic eye reflecting streams of light back at their predator.

The D.O.A. Shrimp® was Mark's real success story many years ago. He continues to take it a step further with better balance and leg design for a "live shrimp" swimming action and the plastic body is stuffed with shrimp and baitfish flavor and scent. This lure has successfully fooled almost every species of fish that feed on live shrimp.

The Softshell Crab®, also stuffed with shrimp and baitfish flavor, has caught everything from red drum, permit, to tarpon and snook. It has great lifelike swimming action when retrieved slowly. I have seen redfish dive on this thing when they were not interested in anything else!

On the Internet, contact D.O.A. at http://www.doalures.com for more information.

4.) I always thought a jig was a jig until I met Captain Hank Brown and his HOOKUP Lures® in Islamorada. In the world of jigs, including bucktails and plain jig heads, these HOOKUP Lures® are miles above the rest and have become the most respected product in their class. They are made with strong stainless steel hooks with a perfectly designed head that allows for an upright hook retrieve, enhancing the weed-

less characteristics. The head has three coats of baked vinyl finish with a final clear coat which seals the reflective eyes on the bucktail jigs. The hook eye is even drilled open and you never have to worry about the eye being plugged with paint. I have never seen such a beautiful, high quality jig.

The plain jig head, combined with a live shrimp, is probably the most dependable fish catcher in the Keys and Florida Bay. All of the popular Keys species regularly fall for this deadly combo. Depending on the species you are after, some jig colors seem to attract more strikes than others. Talk to a local tackle shop to see which color is hot during that month.

The bucktail jigs are beautifully tied with hand select, evenly stacked, bucktail, enhanced by a fine hackle feather. These jigs are the next best thing to a hand tied fly. On light tackle they provide a subtle presentation for the spin fisherman. My brother-in-law caught his first bonefish on the white bucktail pattern pictured. He's a believer in the HOOKUP family.

5.) These Check Point® pliers by Donnmar Enterprises will change the way you look at pliers. I always thought that a rusted pair of pliers from Pakistan, that seized up when you needed them, was just part of life on the water. Who would have thought that you could have a pair of luxury pliers!

Mashing down barbs on hooks has become a standard procedure with me, especially with flies, for personal protection, and even jigs when I get into a school of trout or jacks that need to be frequently released.

These world class stainless steel pliers make it easy. They are constructed with a nickel plated sleeve bearing so they will never freeze up. The integral rubber handles are warm to the touch and

occasionally rubbing the gel-coat and saying, "God, I love my Hewes!"

*Bonefish caught by Brian Lightle of Melbourne, Florida.*
Photo by Derek Busby.

provide a slip-proof grip. With a spring loaded return to open the jaws and replaceable tungsten-carbide line cutters, these are truly the Rolls Royce of pliers.

## Back Cover

I can't say enough about my Hewes skiff. In my opinion they make the finest flats boats on the water. The hull design is superb and offers a dry, smooth ride through the chop. With an eight inch draft, this boat has transported my family and friends into mystical places throughout Florida. My son and I have dreamed of owning a Hewes for years. We realized that dream in 1994. Since there is absolutely no wood used in the construction, we expect to continue living that dream for many years.

In Carl Hiaasen's book "Double Whammy" a character in the opening scene is in his garage rubbing the gunwales of his metalflake fiberglass bass boat, professing to love his boat more than his wife, kids, girlfriend and even life itself. I wouldn't go that far, but, since my boat permanently resides in the garage, and I know my wife reads Hiaasen's books, I'll let her catch me

# How to Use This Guide

The "Fishing Guide to the Upper Keys and Florida Bay" is a practical field manual and reference book for fishing the shallow waters surrounding the southern tip of Florida. For those visiting the area, the chapters on techniques and the different fish species will provide basic direction to increase your rate of fishing success. Hopefully everyone, old timers included, will read the sections on seagrass and fishing etiquette.

The real utility of this fishing guide is the collection of color aerial photographs which reveal the submerged grass flats, pot holes, basins, shoals, banks and keys (all the tiny emerged islands). It will take some time and experience to effectively learn how to interpret the color aerials. By exploring new areas and correlating conditions with the aerial photo for that area, a technique will be developed which will allow the angler to plan ahead for specific fishing trips.

Many of the aerial photos give the impression that there are significant land masses throughout the bay. Yet when you venture across the water you will only see expanses of open water. That is because most of the apparent land masses in the photos are actually submerged bottom features. The water in much of the southern bay and area around the Keys is crystal clear which enables the aerial camera to see straight through the water. Take the time to learn how to differentiate between sandy bottom, grassy bottom and true islands in the photos.

The adjoining page is a black and white version of one of the aerials which has been specifically labeled to help you distinguish some of the features mentioned above. Use this photo as a sample guide to get started learning how to interpret aerial photography.

You will find that the photos of northern portions of the bay change in appearance. That is due to the cloudy water conditions, which you can read about in the chapter "The Florida Bay Story." These photos are labeled with additional remarks to help you overcome the inability to see the true bottom.

The color aerial photos are labeled with significant landmarks and popular locations for catching many of the favorite fish species. As you well know, fish can be found at certain times just about anywhere throughout this immense area. Do not restrict yourself to the labeled areas. Explore! Seek out your own private hot spot.

Before a fishing trip, turn to the index maps which precede the color aerials, and select the aerial numbers which cover the territory where you will be fishing. There are 24 aerial photos covering the Keys and Florida Bay area in this book, numbered 1 through 24. Turn to the corresponding aerial photo for your fishing area. Study the features of the area and the recommended hotspots.

Pay particular attention to submerged flats and cuts going through them. Look for long edges of banks where fish tend to run when they are on the move. Also look for the island masses (keys) which offer fishable shoreline.

9

Look at a tide table and determine when to fish the flooded shallows and mangrove shorelines. Plan accordingly by establishing specific times during your outing when you should leave a flat and begin fishing cuts, channels or the deeper edges.

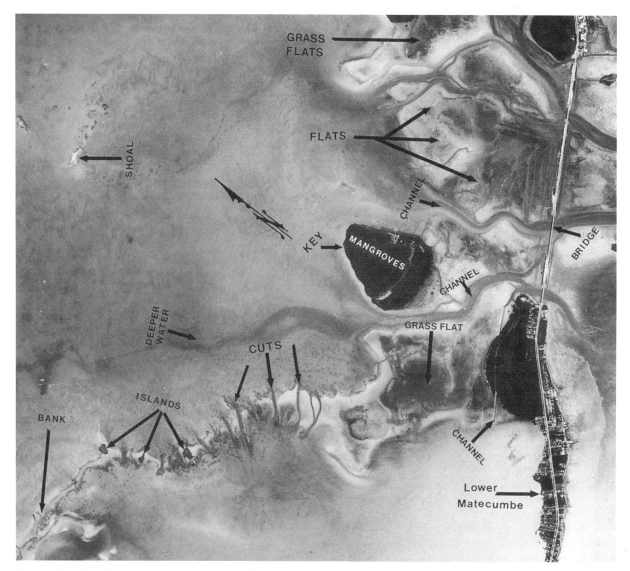

*Example of aerial photo, Lignumvitae Key area.*
All aerial photos acquired from NOAA.

Boaters should check local laws before proceeding. Observe posted speed zones and non-combustion use areas. It is recommended that NOAA and USCG charts be used for navigational purposes.

# Introduction

There just isn't any other place in the country where a better stage is set for saltwater fishing, than the Florida Keys and Florida Bay. The Upper Keys and the bay offer some of the best shallow water fishing opportunities to be found anywhere. An additional bonus to the fishing is the chance to see a wide variety of wildlife found only in this tropical corner of Florida. Some of the spectacular sights may include American Crocodiles, sea turtles, dolphins, sharks, bald eagles, roseate spoonbills, flamingos, ibises and skimmers.

*Ibis feed on an early morning oceanside flat in the Keys.*
Photo by Martin Smithson.

Some call this area the "Sportfishing Capital of the World," some call it paradise. The variety of great fish haunts is practically endless and could consume a lifetime pursuing them all. Oceanside flats, coral patches, backcountry grass flats, mangrove islands and shorelines, cuts and potholes provide a wonderful mix of habitats where fish can most always be found. Even the local bridges produce record gamefish.

Fishing the Keys is incredibly diverse. Within sight of U.S. 1 bridges, on both the bayside and oceanside, one can sample tarpon, bonefish, permit, not to mention the snappers and other small fish available. Run 20 minutes into the shallow backcountry, and trout, redfish and snook are added to the list. If you choose to run 20 minutes in the opposite direction, from the bay to the Atlantic reefs, the quarry changes to bottom fish, and king mackerel, barracuda, amberjack, dolphin and sailfish, to name a few.

Once you enter the Keys area below Florida City, on U.S. 1, the next 20 miles will take you across the northeast corner of Florida Bay, across Key Largo, the largest of the Keys. Some of the best inside trout waters are found here, along with exceptional bonefish flats on the oceanside.

A short distance down the highway is world renown Islamorada. Islamorada area extends from Tavernier Creek on the northeast, to the Long Key bridge on the southwest, encompassing Long Key, Upper and Lower Matecumbe, Windley and Plantation Keys.

In 1903, Henry Flagler started his railroad from Miami to Key West. Flagler's railroad bridged channels, filled swamps and cut through jungles. This seemingly impossible task had the most long-lasting influence on the Florida Keys, most of which is still evident today.

After Hurricane Donna in 1960, the islands blossomed with new marinas, dive shops, motels, restaurants and homes.

It was during the 1960's and '70s that the number of professional fishing guides grew with the increasing demand of visitors seeking world record gamefish.

For years, the endless variety of fishing around the Keys has attracted U.S. presidents, ballplayers, writers and TV personalities. Some of the legendary personalities who came to fish were Presidents Hoover, Truman, Carter and Bush and baseball greats, Lou Gehrig and Ted Williams. Gehrig and Williams were well known for their competitive spirit in the local fishing tournaments.

*Rob Smithson caught his first bonefish on this Islamorada oceanside grass flat.*
Photo by Martin Smithson.

Williams even bought a home in Islamorada, for one reason—fishing.

Today there are more than 150 backcountry guides and 400 offshore captains and mates concentrated in a 10-mile stretch around Islamorada. More than 500 International Game Fish Association world fishing records have been broken in this area and throughout the Keys. Many more are waiting to be broken.

More than 50 annual tournaments in the Keys target bonefish, permit, tarpon, sailfish and dolphin. The tarpon ranks as the heavyweight superstar, with many of the so-called "silver kings" pushing 200 pounds. And the big tarpon attract such big names in sportfishing as Billy Pate, Stu Apte and Chico Fernandez.

Of all the fish found around the Keys, the bonefish attracts the largest following. Considered the "ghost of the flats" because of its lightning speed and disappearing acts, these fish are revered and respected by anglers everywhere.

An expedition north, away from the popular bonefish flats, will take you into the wilderness of uninhabited keys and mangrove shorelines of Florida Bay. Beautiful scenery, plentiful birdlife and superb fishing make this the ultimate backcountry adventure. Many anglers make this trip across Florida Bay to Flamingo. Flamingo is the southern-most point on the Florida peninsula and overlooks the Everglades National Park.

This guide should provide enough information to improve one's ability to find and catch fish in the Keys and Florida Bay area. Whether a weekend visitor who just wants to fish from a bridge or wade a flat, or a professional guide who needs to learn more about the underwater features, the color aerial photos found in this book will be an invaluable tool to help master fishing in the Florida Keys.

# Easy on the Grass Flats

Seagrasses are submerged, grass-like plants that inhabit the shallow coastal waters of Florida. Seagrasses are a vital component of Florida's coastal ecology and economy because they provide food and shelter for a tremendous number of marine species. The grasses have the ability to trap sediment particles, control bottom erosion and maintain the clear water conditions in the Keys and bay area which supports such a fantastic fishery.

*Thick grass beds create clear water.*
Photo courtesy of the National Estuary Program.

The seagrasses are the primary reason why the shallow flats of Florida Bay are considered "the cradle of the ocean." More than 70% of Florida's recreational and commercially important fishes, crustaceans, and shellfish spend part of their lives in the bay in association with the seagrasses. The grassbeds provide a lively nursery for hatched eggs, larvae (immature forms) and juveniles, many of which originated from offshore ocean spawning. Tides and currents carry the swarms of rich, new life into the shallow grassbeds where they can hide and grow until becoming adults when many return to the ocean.

Shrimp, for example, spawn offshore. The developing larvae move toward inshore waters, growing and molting along the way. As young shrimp they burrow in the sandy sea bottom in oceanside waters. On an incoming tide the small shrimp ride into the bay searching for protective seagrasses to hide from predators. Once the shrimp approach maturity, they leave the bay for the sea to spawn, and the cycle begins anew.

An abundant and diverse group of animals inhabit the grassbeds and provide an important link to the higher predators that we as fishermen actively pursue. Cruising over shallow flats in a boat, the grassbeds are easily overlooked as simply dark patches of vegetation. A closer, magnified inspection reveals a fantastic network of plants and animals. Thousands of different species of invertebrates, such as amphipods (water and sand fleas), worms, shrimp, crabs and snails, busily inhabit the grass bed, giving the appearance of a small scale model tropical rain forest. With such an abundant smorgasbord of food items, no wonder many species of fish associate themselves with the grassbeds. Many studies and reports confirm that grassbeds have a higher density and species richness of fishes than adjacent bare sand areas. Fish population studies and inventories have documented several species which are abundant in seagrass beds and feed on the small invertebrates associated with seagrass. Some of the most common ones representing five families of fish, include:

| | |
|---|---|
| Sheepshead | Pigfish |
| Silver Perch | Grunts |
| Red Drum | Porgy |
| Sailors Choice | Spot |

13

Mojarra          Croaker
Gobies           Pinfish
Spotted Sea Trout

This is no doubt an attractive menu for a hungry large predator like the seatrout. The spotted seatrout is one species which spends its entire life cycle associated with the grassbeds in the backcountry bay area.

Having worked with several environmental education programs has provided the opportunity to conduct field trips to grass flats to sample for demonstration purposes. There's nothing that gives a greater appreciation of a grassbed for children and adults than pulling a seine net through knee deep water and sorting the catch. It's not uncommon to capture fingernail size snapper, grouper, trout, and redfish, seahorses, permit, kingfish, spadefish, flounder and barracuda. The experience is something everybody should have at least once.

The productivity of seagrass beds, directly or indirectly provides food for many animals, rivaling that of agricultural crops such as corn and wheat. To maintain their high productivity, however, seagrasses require intense levels of sunlight. Thus, they are dependent on relatively clear water. In deeper water the suspended particles of silt and algae scatter the sunlight to a point where there is not enough light penetrating the depths to support seagrass growth.

Marine-habitat degradation in Florida is continuing at an alarming rate as the coastal residential population and the

number of seasonal visitors increase. Habitat degradation has many sources (e.g. pollution, dredge and fill), but an increasingly common cause of habitat loss is the scarring of seagrass beds.

*Bonefish and permit search for food that hide in turtle grass beds.*
Photo by Martin Smithson.

According to a Florida Department of Environmental Protection Technical Report on Seagrasses: Seagrass beds can be scarred by many activities, but scars are most commonly made when a boat's propeller tears and cuts up roots, stems, and leaves of seagrasses, producing a long, narrow furrow devoid of seagrasses. Boats operating in shallow waters are severely scarring, and sometimes completely denuding, seagrass beds throughout the state.

Small cuts from boat propellers can take two to seven years to recover in a mature, healthy grassbed. More extensive damage from chronic and/or large-scale prop dredging may take decades to recover (Durako et al., 1993).

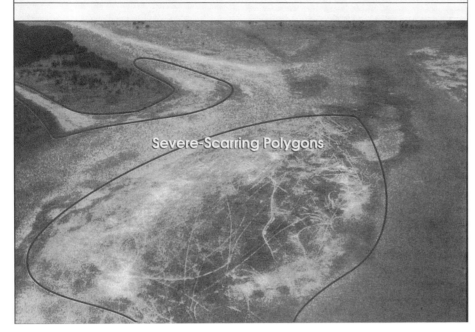

*Prop scars from boats have all but destroyed this flat near Windley Key.*
Courtesy of Florida Department of Environmental Protection.

than any other area of the state. This same area also lays claim to the greatest number of areas which have been scarred by boat props, over 30,000 acres.

The reasons why grass flats get scarred and damaged are when one or more of the following situations occur:

- when boaters mis-judge water depth and accidentally run across the seagrass bed;
- when boaters who lack navigational charts or the skill to use them stray from poorly marked chan-nels and scar adja-cent grass beds;

Durako also states: "Although most scarring by props occurs when boat operators mis-judge water depths, another cause of scar-ring is that the proliferation of "flats" fish-ing boats and other small vessels with hydraulic-trim controlled outboards has resulted in increased boat traffic over shal-low areas that frequently contain seagrass beds. Cumulative damage to seagrass beds in some localized areas is often deliberately caused by boaters who routinely take "short cuts" across shallow flats."

In the Florida Keys, as waterfront and recreational development has increased since the 1970s, so has the number, size and power of vessels in this region - resulting in widespread, and in some cases severe, scar-ring of shallow seagrass communities.

Monroe County alone, which includes Florida Bay and the Keys, contains 55 per-cent of all Florida seagrass-bed acreage. This area has about 1.5 million acres of grass flats which is about 10 times greater

Photo by Martin Smithson.

- when boaters intentionally leave marked channels to take shortcuts through shallow grass beds;
- when boaters carelessly navigate in shallow areas because they think scars heal quickly;
- when boaters overload their vessels, causing deeper drafts than they realize;
- when boaters intentionally prop-dredge to create a channel; and
- when inexperienced boaters, unaware of the value of seagrasses, operate with a disregard for the fishery environment.

What can we do to better protect this wonderful fishing habitat? Become an informed boater. Read pamphlets, attend seminars and classes, use guides and maps and communicate with local agencies, tackle shops and anyone with knowledge of the local areas.

Learn to read the channel markers and stay within the channels where possible. The channel-marking system used by the Everglades National Park has directional arrows and is beginning to help reduce the number of groundings.

Learn to read the water color and it's relation to depth. If it's blue, pass on through. Green should be clean and if it's brown you'll run aground.

Watch for posted areas. Popular grass flats in the Keys have been posted as "Non Combustion Use" which means - turn the outboard off and tilt the motor up. These areas should be poled or trolled (with an electric motor) only.
The vegetation on the bottom (seagrass) is extremely important for maintaining the popular sportfish populations and the beautiful water clarity. Go easy on the grass flats and protect them for the future.

# Sport Fishing Etiquette & Ethics

Having your own secret fishing hole is a rare phenomenon today. Chances are pretty good that someone else knows about your hotspot and fishes it regularly. The trick to maintaining a fishing advantage over the next guy is to know more spots than they do. In addition, one must develop a tolerant attitude and a whole lot of patience.

*Anglers can fish the same vicinity if they pole in quietly.*
Photo by Martin Smithson.

Tolerance is needed for those that recreate on the water and are oblivious to your stealth and stalking skills demonstrated as you pursue wary fish. Patience is needed to find an undisturbed fish haunt where the fish don't have the jitters.

In Florida there are over three million saltwater anglers searching for fish. Fortunately, not all of them fish at the same time. Projections for the state's angling population are scary if you are a fish but promising if you sell boats, bait and tackle.

The number of resident saltwater anglers in Florida is expected to grow by 55 percent by the year 2010. The number of fishing tourists are expected to grow twice as fast.

In a few years your favorite fishing spot may be shared by many. In order for us and the resource to survive, anglers must follow a code of fishing ethics and etiquette.

Just following the rules is not going to be enough. If every angler took one average legal redfish (4 pounds), the entire inshore stock would be wiped out. There is nothing wrong with occasionally taking home a reasonable number of fish to eat. The attitude that must prevail, however, in order to sustain the fishery, is one of limiting our take versus taking our limit.

Floridians have become more conservation minded and now promote a catch-and-release ethic. Sport and gamefish are much more valuable to the local economy when they can be fought on fishing tackle more than once. With the blossoming number of visiting anglers it is important that they adopt the practices of the ethical angler, too. Fishing ethics involves a lot more than just releasing fish. A well rounded angler will be able to:

- Identify most of the species commonly caught in the area.
- Understand the local laws and limits.
- Use the proper techniques for releasing unwanted fish.
- Appreciate the value of habitats and the importance of their protection.
- Observe boating regulations and be conscious of the boat's wake and its effect on other anglers, anchored boats, swimmers and shorelines.
- Respect other anglers and not crowd or disrupt them when they are on another spot.
- Keep personal debris and litter from entering the waterways.
- Share fishing expertise with others.

17

*Brian Lightle of Melbourne, Florida drew a crowd when he hooked a big bonefish on this oceanside flat.*
Photo by Martin Smithson.

Entering a bay or flat under the power of an outboard motor does not create a very pleasing atmosphere in a fish's underwater sanctuary. Guides in the Florida Keys have learned that their success rate for large fish is much greater when drifting or poling in shallow areas.

The use of a push pole has allowed several anglers to fish a flat together while quietly maneuvering their boats. While electric trolling motors are much quieter than gas powered outboards, most guides prefer to use the push pole method. This quieter stalking technique is more critical when approaching species such as tarpon, permit and bonefish.

As the fishing grounds become more and more crowded, it is equally important that anglers learn to get along with each other in addition to protecting and preserving the resource.

Probably the most important rule to remember when practicing the etiquette of fishing with others is—Approach Quietly. Sound travels through water four times more efficiently than through air. Noise is something that must be kept in mind when approaching fish or passing the vicinity of someone else fishing.

Fish become aware of anglers through sensory organs in their head as well as the lateral line along the sides of their body. They are so keen on detecting movements, vibrations and pressure changes that they can detect a small crab crawling along the bottom at night.

Keep in mind that any foreign noise which enters the fish's environment will alert the fish and make them more difficult to catch. A fleeing fish also sends a distinct signal to others, also putting them on notice.

Captain Hank Brown of Islamorada strongly believes that you should follow a simple rule: "Pole in and pole out." In other words, if you take the time to pole onto a flat and finish with your own fishing activity, take the time to pole back out to deeper water before firing up the outboard. This will preserve the fishing conditions for the next guy, or even for yourself if you return later in the day under different conditions.

It is obvious how disruptive an outboard engine must be to a fish. The fish's world is a symphony of soft clicks, gurgles and pops that is easily disrupted by the untimely clash of symbols when, for instance, someone's pocket knife bounces around the cockpit of a boat. The thin fiberglass hull acts like a giant public address system amplifying every thump, rattle and slammed hatch lid throughout the water.

Lefty Kreh, leading fly fishing authority and writer on the subject, believes that even loud talking will alert fish in slick, calm

*Areas like this can be a sanctuary to fish and are no place to run a motor.*
Photo by Martin Smithson.

waters. He has proven his theory by yelling when trout or bonefish were present, only to observe them scoot away. He recommends that anglers carry on conversations in low voices.

I asked Flip Pallot, host of ESPN's "Walkers Cay Chronicles" and veteran Everglades angler for his primary thoughts regarding fishing etiquette and he admonished..."Don't run boats in the fishes' house!!! If you know where fish live or feed, or think you do, don't run or putt in these areas. Use a push pole. Use it more than you think you need to." Pallot goes on to explain, "Populations of fish can be manipulated very easily by fishing pressure, motor noise and the simple presence of foreign activity in their house or neighborhood. Think about the presence of

these factors in your own house or neighborhood. You would be immediately aware and would respond in some way. Fish are at least as aware of these things as we would be, probably more so."

There is another set of behavioral tips that don't really relate to the fish and places they live but to the people you fish with. Some of the following tips apply if you are fishing on a friend's boat, but mostly apply when fishing with a professional guide.

When fishing with a friend or guide, before you step aboard their vessel, be prepared. Spend some time the day before getting ready.

- If fishing with a guide make sure you either have the proper tackle for the fish you will be pursuing, or that you are prepared to use the guide's tackle. Improper tackle is a hassle and takes up valuable space.

- Check with a local tackle shop and purchase the recommended lures or flies, or use what the guide recommends. Don't bring along a box full of lures that you use in another region.

- There is no real dress code, however, it is important to dress comfortably and protect yourself from the elements, mainly the sun. Light cotton material is best. A hat and sunscreen are a must. Regarding foot apparel, it is absolutely critical that you do not wear black-soled shoes. They will leave streaks and scuff marks on the deck and make the owner of the vessel most unhappy. Wear white-soled deck shoes.

- Invest in a pair of top-quality polarized sunglasses. They are essential on the flats. The best color lenses are dark amber or bronze-colored. Without decent glasses the entire flats experience is compromised.

*After a day on the water, time is taken to prepare for the next day's fishing.*
Photo by Martin Smithson.

- Get it square with your guide or friend ahead of time regarding who is responsible for food and beverages. It is extremely important to have the proper liquids to avoid becoming dehydrated. Water or Gatorade® is a necessity.

- As a final suggestion, bring the basics mentioned above but remember to keep paraphernalia to a minimum. Most flats skiffs have limited storage space.

As our fishing territory gets more and more congested as everyone tries to escape the maddening crowd, it is increasingly important that we all give consideration to practicing sportfishing etiquette.

# The Florida Bay Story

## *Florida's Premier Bay is Ailing*

I fell in love with the Florida Keys 20 years ago. Actually, the love affair began over 30 years ago when I first read about and saw photos of the Keys.

The thrill has always been seeing so many different shades of indigo, emerald and turquoise water blend together over the shoals, cuts and channels. Over the years we have begun to explore more of the greener, shallow waters on the north side of the Keys, known as Florida Bay.

Florida Bay is over 900 square miles of hard-bottom shallows, grassy banks and mangrove islands that stretch between the southern tip of the Florida peninsula and the Keys. Over 85 percent of this salty bay lies within the Everglades National Park. The bay is relatively shallow as average depths are less than three feet.

We never ventured far from the Keys, staying within four or five miles of the islands where the water remains clear from the exchange with the Atlantic.

Here it is less obvious that serious problems plague the backcountry of Florida Bay.

For several years there has been a growing environmental focus on the dying Everglades at a state and national level. The river that feeds the backcountry of Florida Bay is the Everglades. Freshwater flows in a sheet across marl prairies of the South Florida sawgrass marshes and through creeks fed by the Taylor Slough and Shark River Slough system.

The freshwater provides the delicate balance of brackish conditions which creates a diverse estuary much like the Indian River system on the east coast. In fact, the target

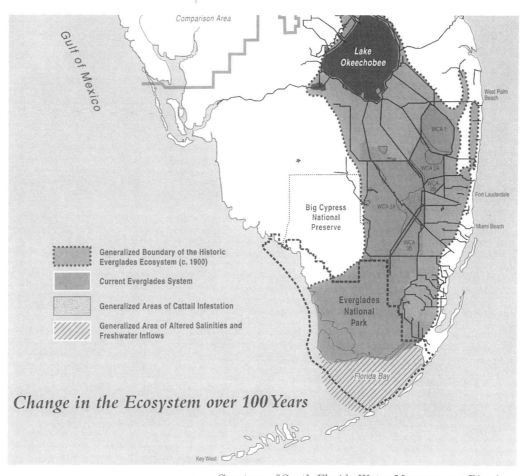

Generalized Boundary of the Historic Everglades Ecosystem (c. 1900)

Current Everglades System

Generalized Areas of Cattail Infestation

Generalized Area of Altered Salinities and Freshwater Inflows

*Change in the Ecosystem over 100 Years*

Courtesy of South Florida Water Management District.

recreational fish species in Florida Bay are very similar to those in other estuaries around the state—snook, tarpon, spotted seatrout and redfish.

The freshwater, which is vital to the Everglades and the bay off Florida's southern tip, is in great demand by south Florida's urban and agricultural interests. And the water that is not used is whisked away by canals and dumped off the east coast for flood control before it has a chance to filter down into the Everglades and the Bay.

In the 1920's, hurricanes killed several thousand people south of Lake Okeechobee. The flood of 1947 was the most severe on record in South Florida when back to back hurricanes flooded 2.5 million acres, leaving standing water for up to six months. In response to public demand for an all-out, no-holds-barred approach to flood control, Congress authorized the Central and Southern Flood Control project in 1948. The construction of levees, canals and pump stations, beginning in 1950, became one of the world's largest plumbing system, "water management" projects. The River of Grass was severely disrupted and cut up in order to provide freshwater and flood control to South Florida.

This alteration of the natural flow of water through the River of Grass compounded by the discharge of nutrients and pollutants from today's intense agricultural and urban land use, is crippling the Florida Bay ecosystem.

The ecosystem of Florida Bay is a significant resource. At least 22 commercial and/or important recreational aquatic species are known to use the bay as a nursery ground. These include young spiny lobsters, several species of snappers, grunts and groupers. Florida Bay and nearby coastal embayments are the principle nursery habitat for pink shrimp which is the basis of a multi-million dollar fishery in the Tortugas. Pink shrimp are an important species commercially and form a food base for predator species.

During the summer of 1987, approximately 100,000 acres of seagrass, known as turtle grass, "died off" in western Florida Bay. This die-off was followed by algal blooms and sponge die-offs. The cause was thought to be from elevated salinity—actually becoming saltier than the ocean—due to the lack of freshwater flowing down through the Everglades.

Conditions within Florida Bay have continued to visibly decline since 1987, including losses of seagrass habitat; diminished water

*Captain Paul Glanville finds schooling fish in the upper reaches of Florida Bay.*
Photo by Martin Smithson.

clarity, long duration algal blooms; and population reductions in economically important species such as pink shrimp, sponges, lobster and recreational gamefish. In addition to these problems, populations of wading birds, forage fish, and juvenile gamefish species have been reduced.

In 1990, massive fish kills added insult to injury as many of the angling clients chose the Bahamas for their pursuit of clear water flats. The effect upon backcountry fishing, a major industry of the Keys, has been dramatic.

These incidents appeared to be shocking signals that the bay was near collapse or already had occurred. Above normal rainfall in 1993 and 1994, however, breathed some life back into the bay. There is hope that a reduction of nutrients and pollutants entering the bay and a basic re-plumbing of South Florida's canal system to restore more natural volumes of freshwater inflow into Florida Bay, will restore the dying system.

A great boost for Florida Bay came in 1994 with the passage of legislation to restore the estuary. The state directed the South Florida Water Management District to modify the quantity, quality, timing and distribution of water delivered to the bay to effect restoration. The Everglades Forever Act specifies that Florida Bay is part of the Everglades Protection Area, and thus must be restored and protected.

The District is working with the U. S. Army Corps of Engineers to establish a series of restoration initiatives which will increase the quantity and quality of fresh water flows to Florida Bay. Meanwhile scientists are busily calculating the necessary mix of fresh and saltwater which is needed to sustain the estuary into the future.

The plan in the coming years is to purchase farms and other altered lands and build berms around 44,000 acres to create one of the largest stormwater projects in the world. The constructed wetlands will reduce nutrients in the runoff which is accelerating the spread of cattails and algae blooms in the marshes and bay. According to one official with the U.S. Army Corps of Engineers, "the restoration and replumbing of South Florida will have as profound an influence on the state as the construction of the original system almost 50 years ago."

For those that wish to see the real wilderness of the Everglades National Park and Florida Bay, a trip to Flamingo at the southern tip of the mainland Florida peninsula is in order.

For more information about Florida Bay and the Flamingo area, read the chapter "Fishing Flamingo" in this book, or call the Flamingo Lodge at (941) 695-3101.

# Personal Notes

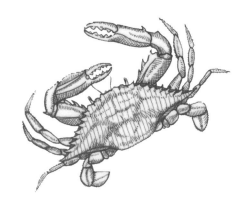

# Shallow Water Fishing Techniques

The string of islands known as the Florida Keys are surrounded by shallow oceanside grassflats to the south and a shallow bay to the north. These shallow waters, often referred to as "flats," provide some of the most unique fishing opportunities in North America.

This book focuses on the shallow areas of the Keys. Offshore, or deep sea fishing is another exciting and challenging world where anglers travel to nearby waters over a 1,000 feet deep searching for dolphin, sailfish, marlin and wahoo. Those that are new to the sport may choose to take a party boat out to 100 feet of water and fish the bottom structure for a wider variety of fish including grouper and many types of snapper. There are many charter boats available for the deep sea fishing adventures. If you want deep water, inquire at the local marinas for descriptions of the offshore adventures available.

The backcountry is an entirely different game compared to offshore. Gliding along in two feet of crystal clear water, one can easily become lost in the silence. Observing the grass flats and the life they contain makes the search enjoyable even if you don't catch many fish. Most of the fishing is done by sight, looking for the actual fish or their signs such as ripples and wakes as they move around.

Fishing the backcountry can be difficult if you are a novice angler. The best advice is to employ a licensed guide and learn some basic approaches. It is worth the investment to get to know a guide and fish with them regularly. For a few hundred dollars over several trips you will instantly pick up years of valuable experience. A guide is almost essential when learning to fish the Keys because of the many variables that must be considered. The guide is in tune to the movement patterns of the fish, the time of day and locations where they are active, the wind, water clarity, temperature, etc., etc. A visiting angler cannot possibly be knowledgeable of these important factors during a short visit.

This chapter will discuss some basic and general techniques to get a person started in the right direction to catch fish in the Keys. There are other publications written by long-time professionals that go into much greater depth and detail regarding fishing techniques. With today's variety of tackle

*Don Perchalski chases Brian Lightle's 100 lb. tarpon hooked on ten pound tackle in two feet of water. The high speed excitement lasted 10 minutes.*
Photo by Martin Smithson.

and equipment a treatise would have to be written in order to cover all the possibilities. The topic of fishing line, for example, has become more of a science than a sport due to the introduction of so many different materials. We will try to touch on just enough to start catching fish!

## Tackle & Equipment

On a recent trip to the Long Key area I stopped to observe several anglers fishing under the Channel 5 bridge. Their

*One of the most effective rigs in the Keys is a HOOKUP jig and live shrimp.*
Photo by Martin Smithson.

tackle consisted of large heavy surf rods, heavy line, coated wire leader with snap swivels, three to four ounces of lead and 3/0 to 4/0 hooks. I watched as they killed a few shrimp, impaling them with the large hooks. One gentleman walked over and asked if I had any tips for them as they had never fished in the Keys before. I gave the man a 3/8 ounce HOOKUP jig and convinced him to try it on his lightest rod without the wire leader. We pinched the tail off of a shrimp, so it wouldn't spin in the current and hooked it onto the jig. The man cast near the base of a concrete piling and instantly his rod bent double and his line went snap. He turned to me with wide eyes and asked, "Where can I buy some jigs like that?"

Bridge fishing creates somewhat of a dilemma in that you need stout enough tackle to horse the fish out of the pilings but light enough terminal tackle to draw a strike. Typically around bridges a good 15 pound spinning outfit or a 20 pound plug casting outfit is suitable. When fishing for tarpon on the flats these outfits will also fit the bill.

The trend for many anglers today is to go even lighter with the tackle. Especially since shallow water flats fishing is mostly a sight fishing activity. The lighter tackle allows for better accuracy and a quieter undetected approach.

My experiences as a youngster were either from ocean piers, bridges, surf or deep-sea bottom fishing. The "heavy duty" philosophy carried over for a number of years. If I could find a huge, oversized spinning reel on a big rod, at a cheap price, I'd jump on it. My greatest pleasure over the past few years has been seeing those outfits go to the garage sale or to the dump. It took years to figure out that reels made from inexpensive materials will not last and will not perform when that "once in a lifetime" strike occurs.

When you leave the surf and the pier to head towards the flats it's time to get the lead out. That is, get those pyramid sinker weights out of the tackle box. And you probably won't need those heavy swivels, spreader rigs or attractor beads. The wire leader is not necessary unless you are going after barracuda. So the box of crimps and crimping pliers are also weighting you down. On many trips all you will need is a one layer plastic sectional box for lures, a spool of mono leader, line cutters and needlenose pliers. I can say that my fishing tackle has become much more simplified over the past few years.

The front cover of this book represents what I would term "reliable" and essential equipment. There is tremendous competition today in the tackle market. The lures pictured will catch fish, I've experienced them first hand and have a high level of confidence when using them. There are many others which are similar that may or may not work. You have to build your own collection and confidence level by trying the ones you see or hear about that catch fish. More detailed discussion on the lures pictured is found in a previous section called "About the Cover" and discussed further as related to specific species throughout this book.

Many professionals today will tell you that the most important piece of equipment is the fishing line—the one thing between

angler and fish that must be in perfect condition. With the more frequent use of lighter lines, condition is extremely important to land fish. While line is important, my opinion is that the equipment needed to propel the lure to the right spot is very important. I've seen times when the lure could not have been very important, when a frenzied snook has attacked before it could possibly have known what in the world it was biting. A pop top from a beer can would have surely brought on the same strike. The key here is getting that lure to land where you want it to. The rod and reel have to work together. A good reel on a cheap rod with too few guides can cause problems. A cheap reel on a good rod, likewise. Most of my headaches, heartaches and frustrations have resulted from a fouled up reel. Bails that trip prematurely, loops and birdsnests, drags that stick, handles that flop, fizzled anti reverse, and improperly spooled line, have created some anxiety on several occasions.

Purchase a good balanced outfit that is not too heavy. Today's graphite and new fiberglass materials create some very light but strong rods. Many reels such as the new Penn spinning reels are progressing toward graphite bodies which are light and corrosion resistant. Line capacities for 8–10 lb. test should run from 120 yds., on small reels to 200 yds. or greater on medium size reels. The average rod used on the flats is a 6.5 ft. to 7 ft., medium action, high modulus graphite, rated for 1/4 to 1/2 oz. lures. Fly fishing equipment will be addressed separately in this chapter.

Back to the fishing line. Monofilament line can exhibit many different characteristics from different manufacturers. Factors such as stretch or elongation, diameter, how it reflects light, and whether it is hard or soft, limp or rigid, will affect the performance such as distance and accuracy, and not to mention the ability to fight a fish. If you are going after world line class records then you

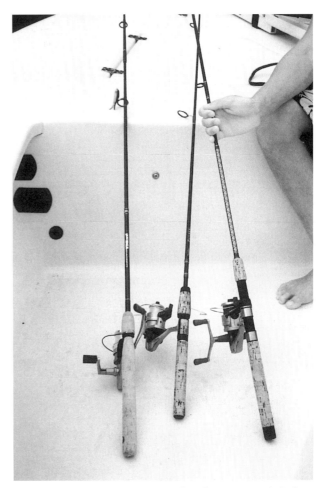

*Shallow water equipment has become much lighter today averaging in the 10 lb. class.*
Photo by Martin Smithson.

need to delve into the technical aspects of monofilament line processing before choosing a brand of line. A good premium brand line used by many Florida guides is made by Ande. I strictly use Ande for line and leader material, most frequently using 8 and 10 lb. test. For leader material I use 20 and 25 lb. test. When fishing for tarpon or around bridges, 15–20 lb test is more appropriate with a 30–40 lb. test leader material.

First, a little information about knots before discussing the shock leader. There are so many different knots that entire publications are devoted to them. When saltwater fishing, it won't take long to realize that the old fisherman's knot you learned as a kid is no longer good enough. A feisty little snook or redfish will pull that knot right out. That's exactly what prompts most anglers to learn new knot tricks. There are three good knots worth learning which are very reliable and should hold up under most situations. The Bimini Twist creates a section of doubled line to which the leader can be attached. It provides strength and acts as a shock absorber. The Double Surgeon's knot is an easy and effective way to connect two pieces of monofilament. This knot is very strong for tying the heavier leader to the doubled line which was created by the Bimini Twist. You can also connect two single pieces of mono if you choose not to use the Bimini Twist. The result will be less shock absorbing action. For tying lures or flies to the end of the leader the Uni-knot is superb. This knot also allows the flexibility of creating a loose loop for greater lure or fly action. When pressure is applied, the knot will slide up tight against the hook or lure eye. This knot is very similar to but stronger than the improved Clinch Knot. It is recommended that a copy of *Baits, Rigs and Tackle* by Vic Dunnaway be purchased at a local tackle shop and at a minimum, learn the three knots mentioned above.

There is a delicate balance between using a light enough leader which goes unnoticed, drawing more strikes, and using one heavy enough to hold up against slashing teeth, sharp gill plates, abrasive bodies, mangrove branches and bridge pilings. Some trout and bonefish anglers do not use a shock leader, trying to fool the big ones which seem to be more wary. For other species, such a snook and barracuda you need to have a piece of heavier leader material if you want to avoid being cut off.

## Lures & Bait

With regard to what one should use on the end of a line to catch fish, more detail is provided in the individual sections covering popular Keys and Florida Bay species. We can't possibly cover all the possible lures, plugs, flies and baits that are available in the

Keys but, there are several good books available at tackle shops and book stores, which are dedicated to this topic.

Live baits vary during the year and are mainly used to target the giant tarpon moving through the channels. It may be mullet, pinfish, crabs or shrimp drawing the most strikes. It is best to check with your guide or local tackle shops to find out the fare of the week.

Most live baits can be purchased at many of the local bait and tackle shops or marinas. You will need a recirculating live-well in your boat or you can purchase various sized aerated bait buckets. Another option for obtaining bait is to learn how to throw a cast net. This takes practice and still requires one to be pretty savvy at finding schools of bait.

Pinfish and mullet are excellent bait to use for tarpon and snook around the channels and bridges. Pinfish can be easily collected from the flats by throwing out some frozen chum and then fishing for the pinfish with small hooks (#10 or #12) tipped with a piece of shrimp suspended from a small cork float. You can catch enough to fill a live-well and have a little fun doing it, especially if kids are included.

Captain Hank Brown likes to hook the pinfish through both lips and drift them about four feet below a float around the passes. He says that the float technique is important because the tarpon are always near the bottom with all eyes looking up. Always keep the live bait above their looming predator.

In the fall of the year, Captain Brown will fill his live-well with 200 to 300 pilchards (a large sardine) and head for the backcountry channels in Florida Bay. He will anchor near a cut through one of the banks (Ninemile Bank for instance) and

*The D.O.A. TerrorEyz simulate bait fish which tarpon blast under the bridges.*
Photo by Martin Smithson.

chum with some of the pilchards. Using a HOOKUP jig he hooks a pilchard through the mouth and tosses out to hungry mangrove snapper. He uses this technique to catch the really big snapper.

The artificial lures pictured on the cover of this book represent some of the most basic items needed to catch a wide variety of fish in the Keys. You just can't beat a bucktail jig or the combination of bucktail and feathers in a fly. The D.O.A. soft baits are guaranteed effective. The new TerrorEyz is surprisingly effective on tarpon under the bridges and the 3″ and 4″ shrimp are all-time favorites. For someone who just simply wants to catch fish, there is probably no better combination than a jig head and a live shrimp. The HOOKUP jigs (pictured on the cover) have accounted for every species mentioned in this book. From big snook around Flamingo to tarpon on the flats, the shrimp and jig won't be beat.

## Finding the Fish

Flats fishing around the Keys and Florida Bay is as much like hunting as it is fishing. Learning all the different conditions which fish should be found in, and the signs which give away their presence, adds an exciting element to sportfishing. The thrill of sight fishing on the flats can only be equaled, at best, by wild game hunting in the woods.

Over the years I have become more sensitive to the signs of fish. Sometimes the alertness pays off, other times it results in wasted time and energy when a glimpse of a submerging cormorant, flapping ray, gasping turtle or school of mullet sends me off in a frenzied search for the trophy fish conjured up in my mind. The effort is not really a waste because the myriad of wildlife seen along the way is pure delight.

One of the most important tools to an angler in the Keys, in addition to the fishing tackle, is a good pair of polarized sunglasses. They will cut the glare and not only allow you to see fish more clearly, but also allows you to see the bottom features. It is easy to identify the angler who is without good glasses on the boat. It's the angler who misses all the action and keeps asking—"Where? What fish? I can't see it."

Plan on spending between $100 and $150 for a good pair of glass lens constructed glasses. This may sound outrageous for sunglasses. For many years I scoffed at the notion of paying very much for glasses. This is until I experienced the difference in wearing a premium brand. Today I would panic if I lost my glasses and would scrape up the money somewhere to replace them.

*Without polarized sunglasses, as in the top photo, big tarpon cannot be seen lurking below, as in the bottom photo.*
Photos by Martin Smithson.

an excellent conductor of sound, and the hull of a boat acts as a huge stereo speaker with a traveling band. Every little bump of a reel against the gunnels, a kicked anchor chain, a slammed deck lid or a dropped pocket knife is amplified through the water. And believe me, your audience is very attentive to the signals they receive in their environment. Too many suspicious bumps and clicks will send that keeper redfish sliding off the flat and into an unreachable location. The professionals you see poling today's flats boats are not doing it for sport or style, they are poling to increase the chances of having their client hook up with an unsuspecting fish. I've proved it to myself by poling up to a flat from 200 ft. out and catching fish on the first cast, and motoring up to a flat and not getting a hit. You don't necessarily have to have a $300 push pole and a poling platform. Many small shallow draft skiffs can be eased along with a closet rod. The bottom line is that the extra effort given to make a quiet approach is worth it.

The Ocean Waves® line are some of the best quality sunglasses found in Florida. The optical quality reduces eye strain and provides great contrast enhancement in all light conditions. Combined with a good hat, nothing can escape your sights.

## Approach

The approach to your selected fishing spot is most important. Some species of fish are very sensitive to a sudden intrusion into their aquatic world. Water is

The next best way to approach an area, besides poling, is to use an electric trolling motor. Trolling motors become a necessity when weaving in and out of dock-lined shores. Many claim that the electric motors

*Poling a skiff can be a lot of work, but usually pays off.*
Photo by Martin Smithson.

don't spook the fish. I have been told that when using an electric motor the fish are less shy when using a constant speed versus switching back and forth. Use a premium trolling motor in the Keys, one that is designed for saltwater if possible. An inexpensive electric motor will only last a year in the salt.

## Sight Fishing Versus Blind Casting

Nothing is more exciting than seeing the fish you are after, and enticing that fish to strike with a calculated cast. In order to sight fish, the conditions don't always have to be exactly like those crystal clear tropical conditions that you see on the televised programs. You can learn to anticipate a fish's actions by just watching the swirls and occasional exposed dorsal and tail fin. This is still sight fishing when you are responding to the different signs. Most of the time in the Keys, clear water conditions allow for some spectacular sight fishing, particularly near the bridges and channels and on the ocean side flats. Without polarized sunglasses you will have a difficult time seeing any fish. They are an absolute necessity.

And again there is no comparison between a premium brand and a cheap imitation.

Many times in Florida Bay you will be faced with cloudy conditions which prevent you from seeing the bottom or the fish, especially during windy days. When you go to one of the charted fish producing areas and don't see any signs of fish, you will have to resort to blind casting or long, search-type casts. Many backcountry anglers have developed a methodical way of fishing when blind casting. Whether using a streamer on fly gear or top water plugs on conventional tackle, an area should be peppered with casts. Each cast should dissect the area like cutting a pie, with each cast being placed 10 to 15 feet apart. If there is a fish in the area, it will see or hear the lure. The casting and retrieving may become somewhat mechanical and slow but it pays off.

## Setting the Hook

Hooks must be sharp. What looks and feels sharp may actually be dull when examined under a microscope. New hooks which rattle around in a box can become dulled. It is recommended by almost every guide to sharpen every hook with a file, even new ones out of the pack. For some species such as tarpon, with a hard mouth, the barb is filed down to allow for easier penetration. Some guides make it a habit to file down the barb regardless of the species. This is based on the belief that if a fish is played properly, the barb is not necessary to hold the hook in place. A barbless hook also allows an easier release, is less damaging to the fish, and most importantly, barbless hooks result in fewer trips to the emergency room which interrupts a good day of fishing.

One of the most consistent errors made by anglers is striking too soon. When a fish takes a lure or bait, they must first expel the water out through the gills before they try to swallow the bait or lure. A pause before setting the hook enables them to do this. Some fish such as

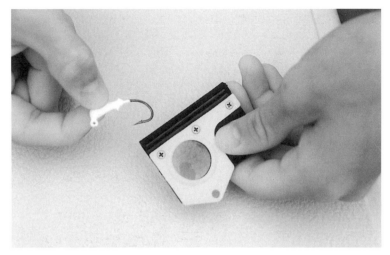

*Donnmar's deluxe hook sharpener puts a razor point on in seconds with unique carbon steel roller cutters.*
Photo by Martin Smithson.

## Battling a Hooked Fish

The success of the battle is a function of the preparations made before the cast; sharp hooks, good knots and line and most importantly a smooth drag. The drag must be adjusted properly prior to fighting a fish or the fight will be a brief one. Another common angler error is setting the drag too tight. Some guides recommend setting the drag at 15–20 percent of the line test. In other words, if you are using ten pound test, it should only take 1.5–2 pounds of pressure to start the spool turning. You can use a fish scale to set the drag at the proper percentage depending on what strength line you use. The drag should be tested straight off the spool. When the rod is lifted during a fight and bowed, there is more drag created due to the friction of the guides and the bend of the rod. Furthermore, the more line in the water after the fish makes a run imparts even more drag. As the diameter of the spool decreases with less line on it, the drag increases even more. You can see now how quickly these factors add up to exceed the breaking point of the line. You are better off with a lightly set drag which can be increased if needed with hand pressure on the spool or line. *Never tighten a drag while fighting a fish.* You'll be sorry.

Redfish have crushers in the back of their mouths and need time to work the lure towards the back. Otherwise the lure or fly will pop right out.

No matter how you set the hook, the line between the tip of the rod and the fish must be taut, and the tip of the rod should point directly at the fish. The two reasons why you don't want slack line when you strike are (1) a slack line will not supply enough force to set the hook and (2) if the hook does set, the snap of a slack line is more likely to break than the same force on a taut line. In a typical strike, reel in slack line if necessary, point the rod and lift the rod with a series of short, sharp jerks in quick succession. You will have to judge the force of the jerks with the line strength and the species of fish. If you are fishing for tarpon, use great authority. If you are fishing for spotted seatrout, since they have tender mouths, merely lift the rod firmly. Side strikes are more popular. Pulling to the side puts the hook in the side of the mouth instead of the bony upper jaw. Also, if you miss the strike, the lure or bait stays in the vicinity of the fish providing another opportunity. A missed upward strike can result in an unwanted hookup in your own fleshy parts.

Let a fish make the initial run. You will want them to use up that burst of energy. Once they stop, then you'll want to work the fish in as quickly as possible. If you have hooked a leaper, you need to bow to him on every leap. As soon as a fish breaks the surface of the water, push the rod towards the fish stretching forward with your arm and body. The force on the line is much greater in the air than in the water. A jumping fish can shake the hook out more easily against a tight line and break tight line more easily with the sudden pressure increase. When you bow to the fish you are controlling the

*A bonefish is pushed back and forth through the water until it regains enough strength to be released.* Photo by Martin Smithson.

slack line. When the fish is back in the water, regain the slack and continue the fight.

When a fish is brought near the boat, or your body when wading, the fish will spook, dive and dart when seeing you or the boat. Be prepared for this and give them the line. Don't pull back. Many fish are lost at this point. Some people actually loosen the drag when a fish is brought in for the final stage of the fight. Decide ahead of time whether you are going to release the fish or keep it. A landing net is useful in either case.

When releasing a fish, first make sure your hands are wet. Dry hands or rags will remove the slime coat that the fish needs to protect itself. Don't hold a fish around the gills or eyes. Handle the fish firmly and remove the hook. If the hook has been swallowed don't try to pull it out. Cut the leader near the mouth and revive the fish by moving it back and forth slowly in the water, forcing water through the gills. This helps the fish recover more oxygen from the water

to get its strength back. When it regains its strength, it will swim on its own.

## Using the Tides

The best tides for tarpon fishing in the backcountry and for bonefish and permit on the flats are the extreme tides. These tides, also called spring tides, occur twice a month during the full and new moon. As a general rule the best fishing is early and late in the day. Combine this with a low incoming tide, or a high outgoing tide and the activity is usually better. It is a good idea to keep track of the tides and record their stage when you catch fish in a specific location. You can then return to various spots when the tide conditions are repeated.

As a rule of thumb—snook or tarpon fishing in the mouths of passes or channels is best during the first two hours of the outgoing tide and the last hour of outgoing. On the flats, the last hour of outgoing and the first hour of incoming are typically the prime tides to fish.

Tides influencing fish activity depend upon the species and the type of habitat that you are fishing. I have had great enjoyment fishing the backcountry of the Everglades when you could hear snook popping back in the flooded mangroves. As the tide fell, these fish worked their way out and came into reach of my lure. Their feeding ground back in the mangroves literally ran out of water with the outgoing tide. This is a predictable occurrence which happens twice a day.

There are some other general conditions which should be considered when fishing the Keys of the Bay.

- The shallow grass flats will be most productive during higher tides when fish venture up on the flat to search for food.

- Oceanside flats are best on a rising tide. Particularly near the outside edges. As the "top of the tide" approaches, the beach areas and mangrove shorelines are best fished at this tide.

- Bonefish move around significantly with every subtle tidal change. The edges of flats are popular for bonefish on the early rise and the late fall of the tide. They can be found highest on the flat just before the outgoing turn.

- Channels, cuts and deeper potholes throughout the bay are best fished during a falling tide when the water is flowing on its way out. Continue fishing until dead low.

- Bottom fishing is best on a rising tide through high tide. Focus on deep channels at low tide.

- Bridge fishing for tarpon and snook is best on an outgoing tide when the water is flowing from the bay side to the ocean side. During a full moon and a new moon the currents can be too strong and difficult to fish. The best time to fish currents under the bridges is during a quarter moon.

## Fishing the Bridges

When the outgoing tide flows from the bay side out to the ocean side, plenty of shrimp, crabs and mullet are carried through the bridges. This makes the bridges a focal point to fish for tarpon, snook, permit, snapper and a variety of other species.

There are two distinct ways to fish bridges in the Keys: either by land or by boat. Both are very effective approaches. There are some guides that like to fish certain bridges on foot, especially at night.

Here are some pointers when fishing from the land side. First of all, pick your tides. The best tides are around a quarter-moon when they are not too strong. On a full or new moon the tides can really rip through the bridge pilings and make fishing difficult. If the winds are also ripping out of the north or west, forget it, the water will be dirty and moving too fast.

The best rig for fishing the bridges, especially for snook, is a 3/8 oz. HOOKUP lead-head jig, combined with a live shrimp. The most important advice here is on how to fish the jig/shrimp combo. You will most likely see many bridge anglers drifting their lines down current, waiting for a strike. You will also notice a lot of people not catching fish using this technique. The most effective method is to cast up current and slowly, slowly, work the jig back, while smoothly pumping the rod to create the jigging effect and keep the lure just off the bottom struc-

*Ron Merkel of Michigan found some action under the Channel 5 bridge.*
Photo by Martin Smithson.

ture. Let the lure sweep past the base of a piling. The idea is to simulate a natural presentation of bait drifting through the channel. The downside is that you will lose more rigs than the guys with down current stretched lines, but you should experience more explosive strikes.

*The Channel 2 bridge pilings are a famous haunt for Keys tarpon.*
Photo by Martin Smithson.

When you are on foot it is best to fish near the ends of bridges. You will want to work a hooked fish to the side where you can get down to the water's edge to release or retrieve the catch. A large fish being reeled 20 ft. up in the air from the top of a bridge usually ends in disappointment for the angler and the fish.

When night fishing from bridges, avoid shining bright flashlights and lanterns into the water which will certainly scare away the fish and reduce their tendency to bite. Be careful not to disturb someone else's fishing with a flashlight, too.

The most productive bridges in the upper Keys, day or night, seem to be Channel 2, Channel 5, Long Key and Tom's Harbor.

Many other bridges are worth checking out, however.

Fishing the bridges from a boat has advantages over fishing on foot. A boat allows you to cover more area and fish a greater number of pilings. A boat can either be anchored at each selected spot or used to troll parallel to the pilings. Trolling is conducted on the upcurrent side of the bridge using big diving plugs. Trolling is a great technique to use when there are no anglers fishing from the bridge, whose lines may get in the way.

It's a good idea to keep an eye on other boats and see what is generating action. Another popular technique is to drift live pinfish or mullet under a large float. The bait is kept about 3 feet deep. Sometimes a HOOKUP jig will hold the bait at the right depth, versus using a bare, freelined hook with the bait.

Mark Nichols, owner of D.O.A. Lures likes to anchor on the upcurrent side of a bridge and position the stern of his boat within just a few feet of a piling. He then

*Anchor lines must be released quickly when a big tarpon circles a bridge piling and heads for open water.*
Photo by Martin Smithson.

35

uses a green and silver or black and silver 3/8 oz. TerrorEyz lure to cast across current to the next piling. He lets the lures simply drift from the 9 o'clock position to the 12 o'clock position (behind the boat) and holds it there perfectly still. He says most strikes occur at the 11 o'clock position. Mark has caught many tarpon on the TerrorEyz as it is catching on as a great lure under the bridges. He notes that an important point is to keep it still and move slowly which is more representative of natural bait holding in the current.

When fishing under or near bridges, especially for big tarpon, a favorite technique is to anchor and drift back near the pilings. This calls for the use of a quick release anchor line with a float (crab or lobster trap type) tied to the anchor line. If a large fish is hooked, they are sure to head for the pilings on the other side of the bridge. A quick release rig will allow you to toss the anchor line over and pursue the escaping fish. Once the action is over, you can return to the floating anchor line and reclaim your discovered hotspot.

## Fishing the Backcountry— Florida Bay

The Bay area, immediately north of the Keys, is very shallow and difficult to navigate, and is only suitable for shallow draft boats. The only way to learn this area is through experience. The best way to start is by going out with a professional guide. Then you will have a foundation of experience which will allow further exploration into the backcountry.

I have found it to be exhilarating to venture into an unknown area and catch fish. My approach has always been very cautious and conservative, learning an area within three to five miles. The next year when I visit I may venture out another three miles. Just when I

*Fishing the deeper cuts through a shallow flat is a common technique in Florida Bay.*
Photo by Martin Smithson.

get real confident about my local knowledge, I'll discover a hidden shoal, the hard way.

Take several trips to learn the area. Use charts and the aerial photos found in this book. Take notes and take it slow. There are plenty of fish to be caught within a five mile radius of your home base.

There are two standard techniques typically used to fish Florida Bay. Either by poling across and around the shallow flats and banks or by anchoring or staking-out near the edge of a flat and waiting on the fish. Some of these edges are known paths where fish travel, especially tarpon, and will pay off for the patient angler.

Poling allows you to cover more territory and presents a variety of fishing opportunities. Keep a watch out for the deeper depressions which have a lighter colored bottom and cast to these holes. Many times they harbor snook, trout or redfish. Poling the flats in the bay is most productive during the last hour of a rising tide and during the first two hours of a falling tide. When staking out or anchoring near a flat or bank the best fishing is usually during a falling tide.

## Wading

Wade fishing allows you to get close to the fish, witness the strike and experience a real closeness with the fishes' environment. It's a great way to

*Regular dive booties serve as excellent wading shoes on Keys flats.*
Photo by Martin Smithson.

slowly and keep a low profile, you may find tailing fish within spitting distance. I have had fish stand on their nose, grubbing on the bottom, within 15 feet of my legs. So close that casting a fly seemed too awkward. Getting that close is rare in a boat.

The problem with wade fishing in the Keys is access. There are very few wadable, firm bottom flats, which are accessible from the shore and where the access is open to the public. Many privately owned properties, such as hotels and resorts have areas which can be fished on foot. Ask around and check out the bottom features at low tide.

escape the heat by getting wet and a good time to be alone, away from the vacationing crowd. There is probably no better enjoyment to fly fishing than wading an oceanside flat for bonefish in the Keys.

Concerns about sharks and barracudas are not warranted as long as you stay in clear, shallow water. Big fish are easily spooked in these conditions and there have been no attacks on wading anglers that I know of.

Wading offers definite advantages when pursuing the shy bonefish. As long as you move

Wading opportunities are almost nonexistent in the backcountry and around Flamingo. The best spots for wade fishing are for bonefish on the ocean side flats around the Keys. The best bets around Key Largo are from some of the oceanside hotels and their beaches and Harry Harris Park on Key Largo. Along Upper Matecumbe Key there is some limited wading opportunities from hotels. Lower Matecumbe offers some excellent wading flats which are accessible from the road. Some of the best wading can be found around Long Key State Park. Additional wading flats exist around Grassy Key.

Wading does not have to be limited to roadside access. There are endless expanses of good wading flats that are available once you reach them by boat. If you are really keen on wading, you can easily stake out or anchor the boat and slip over the gunwale for some more intimate experiences with the fish and their home.

*There are a few excellent wading areas, next to U.S. Highway 1 around Lower Matecumbe.*
Photo by Martin Smithson.

# Fly Fishing

Saltwater fly fishing is rapidly gaining popularity. The reason is that every species on the flats will eat a fly. Fly fishing can be a deadly technique once you learn the basics. And once learned, many anglers develop an insatiable quest, becoming almost fanatical.

If you get into the wonderful hobby of tying your own flies you will experience great satisfaction when you see a gamefish tear into your own creation. You will also develop a keener interest in furry roadkill victims and craft shops. Today there are more different fly patterns, incorporating more materials, than there are species of fish that eat them. I have learned to tie a few basic patterns and stick with them because they catch fish. My variations are typically related to color. I would say that the Clouser Minnow pattern, a bucktail streamer with weighted lead or brass barbell shaped eyes, is probably the most universal

*Bonefish flies tied with weighted eyes so they will dive quickly to the bottom.*
Photo by Martin Smithson.

and productive fly. According to some of the fly fishing legends, this pattern has caught the most species of fish worldwide.

Fly fishing is not a difficult sport to learn. When I was twelve years old I constructed a resemblance of a flyrod from a two-piece Shakespeare spinning rod, complete with a Martin reel and level line. I really wouldn't call it fly fishing, but I caught a lot of sunfish and bass on popping bugs and convinced myself that I was blazing a new trail. The 30-year plus outfit still hangs on the wall and brings back some humorous memories.

There are numerous books and videos devoted to fly fishing that cover all the details on casting, equipment and fly tying. If you are serious about the sport you probably already have several of these works. The one book that has become the primer for the saltwater fly caster is Lefty Kreh's "Fly Fishing in Saltwater." This is one of the most complete and comprehensive works on fly fishing and is written by one of the most respected authorities in the field. There are other books written by local authorities that cover all the basics of flyfishing such as Captain John Kumiski's "Flyrodding Florida Salt." This book also identifies where-to-go along Florida's coast. Check with your larger, complete tackle shops for these materials to help you learn more about fly fishing.

There are several different types of fly fishing scenarios in the Keys and Florida Bay area. While all are challenging, some are more demanding of tackle and expertise than others. If your target is tarpon, permit or bonefish, you would be wise to charter a professional guide who specializes in these techniques. In the backcountry, particularly around Flamingo, you can have frequent success with trout, snook, redfish, jacks and ladyfish on fly.

*Redfish numbers have increased dramatically in Florida Bay and are now a popular flyfishing target.*
Photo by Chuck Padera.

I asked Flip Pallot, one of the best known fly fishermen around, what species he would recommend for someone just getting started in saltwater fly fishing in the Keys area. He had this to offer, regarding the Florida Bay backcountry, "Redfish, I believe, were specifically designed for the enjoyment of beginning fly fisherfolk. They live in the most beautiful of neighborhoods; they love flies (even poorly presented ones); they're big, pretty to look at, fight well and are wonderful to eat." Flip went on to add some pointers for redfish on fly. He said, "When fishing for redfish remember to position your fly, lure or bait where you think the redfish will be, not where he is." "Allow the fish to encounter your offering rather than to show it to him." The Keys angler can begin to pick up redfish by running five or six miles north into the Florida Bay backcountry.

The basic fly outfit suitable for average Keys fishing is a fast-action (stiff) 8-weight graphite rod with a corrosion resistant, direct-drive reel. The reel should be loaded with at least 200 yards of braided Dacron backing plus a #8 weight-forward floating fly line. The floating line is standard for bonefish on the flats. When fishing the channels and cuts in the Flamingo area for example, a shooting head, sinking line is preferred to keep the fly on the bottom. The sinking line is particularly useful when the water is moving swiftly with the changing tides.

The basic saltwater leader has a butt section of 30-lb. or 40-lb. mono, which can be tied directly to the fly line or attached by serving a loop in the front end of the fly line and looping the end of the mono. This allows for quick interchange of leaders. The class tippet is the lightest section (8-lb. to 15-lb. test for example) and should be at least 15 inches long. A heavier shock tippet of 20- to 30-lb. test is added at the end of the leader for attaching the fly. This piece is usually 12 inches long. Again the references mentioned earlier provide significant detail on the different fly lines and leader construction complete with diagrams of the different knots you will need to know.

If your mission is to tangle with a trophy tarpon on fly, then you should hire a professional guide and use his equipment. The rods and reels are much heavier, 11 or 12 weight, and the leader construction is an exacting science of its own.

Bonefish attract a tremendous amount of attention from fly fishing enthusiasts in the Keys. The fish are large in this area of the world, averaging six pounds, and perform multiple lightening speed runs, exposing the backing on your reel which may not have seen daylight in a good while.

*Steve Morgan of Indian Harbor Beach, Florida enjoys an early morning bonefish flat.*
Photo by Martin Smithson.

My son will attest that I am an absolute authority on this subject.

I vividly remember catching my first bonefish on fly just a few years ago. "Fly Fishing in Salt Waters" magazine featured a Pink Gotcha pattern which I tied only one of on a number 2 hook, the night before we left for the middle Keys. Since I had never really fly fished for bones I was anxious to give this so-called "guaranteed pattern" a try. It was late evening when I waded out onto an oceanside flat in about knee-deep water. The bottom was covered with turtle grass with occasional bare, sandy spots.

I immediately saw something like a school of fish pushing a wake within 50 feet of where I stood. For all I knew it could have been a school of mullet. I cast the small pink-nosed fly out in front and gave some short strips. I felt instant resistance before my fly line began ripping across the flat, quickly disappearing as the fine, white dacron backing began peeling off the reel. There was no doubt what I had lucked into. I was able to retrieve the backing and get several feet of fly line on the reel before the blistering run would be repeated all over again. After four runs the fish tired and I was able to observe and release my first six pound bonefish. Still shaking from the

And surprisingly, bonefish will often readily eat a fly. But of course, you must remember that there are many times when they refuse to even look at a fly.

Wading the oceanside flats in the Keys in search of bonefish provides an excellent opportunity for the novice fly fishing angler to practice their casting skills and still have some reasonable expectation of fishing success. The best times to go are either early in the morning or late in the evening. You are usually alone, there is no pressure from someone scrutinizing your casting errors, you can cast to anything that moves, if you like, and you can still manage in windy conditions without fear of someone getting hurt, with the exception of yourself. Be sure to mash down the barb on every fly with a pair of pliers! While the resulting hump on the hook will sufficiently keep the fly from working loose and falling out of the fish's mouth, the smooth hump will also allow easy extraction from human flesh and avoid costly trips to the emergency room.

experience, and creating great excitement for my teenage son who accompanied me, I proceeded to catch two more bonefish within the next thirty minutes!

Returning to the hotel with the feeling that I had unlocked one of the greatest mysteries of life, a little rum and cigars and constant chatter reliving the event, resulted in a sleepless night and convinced my wife that I was hopelessly hooked.

Confidently, I returned to the same flat, morning and evening, over the next four days. I never saw another bonefish!

On our departure from the Keys I was contemplating on how we could scrape up some quick cash for a return trip. When I suggested holding up a convenience store, my wife replied that the local police would know instantly that it was a "bonefish related robbery." Be careful, flyfishing for bonefish is addicting!

41

# Fishing Flamingo

The Flamingo area is truly one of Florida's unspoiled fishing adventure destinations. Flamingo sits at the southern tip of the mainland Florida peninsula and overlooks Florida Bay. This area provides an opportunity to see the real wilderness of the Everglades National Park.

*Wildlife is abundant in Florida Bay.*
Photo by William Potter.

Many anglers access Flamingo by taking a boat from the Keys across Florida Bay. This trip in itself is a 45 minute to one hour adventure, navigating the backcountry keys, flats and banks. Local knowledge is necessary to cross Florida Bay. The best way to learn the bay is to charter a guide and pay close attention to the charts and aerial photos.

The other way to access Flamingo is by road which leads from Florida City, at the southern end of the Florida Turnpike, southwest through the Everglades National Park. You enter the National Park just outside of Florida City and travel about 40 miles to Flamingo. This route gives you a real appreciation of the magnificent Everglades.

Traveling down Route 27 you will witness a piece of the 1.5-million-acre park that is essentially untouched. The two-lane road traverses thousands of acres of vast sawgrass prairies dotted with stands of bald cypress. Approaching Flamingo the landscape begins to transition into mangrove swamps and subtropical jungles.

This is a beautiful trip that every angler and their family should take at least once. In addition to the visitor's center at the park entrance, there are several nature trails and observation points along the way to Flamingo. This is a trip that appeals to all nature lovers in the family, not just the anglers.

*Park entrance on the road to Flamingo.*
Photo by Martin Smithson.

43

Flamingo is literally the end of the line, but where the fishing begins at Florida Bay. The Outpost Resort is operated by a concessionaire to the Park Service and has just about everything you will need: A marina and store, fuel, launch ramps, slips, boat rentals, lodge, motel, cabins, campground and boat tours. The store is complete with a convenient stocking of food, essentials, tackle, ice and even live shrimp.

Before describing the fishing opportunities —a word of caution is in order. If you and your family take this exciting trip, you must be mentally and physically prepared for the mosquitoes. They are relentless and can get worse than Chinese water torture. Take plenty of spray repellent. Some of the new unscented varieties are more tolerable, especially around the picnic table. Mosquitoes are attracted to carbon dioxide. That is why they will fill up previously occupied vehicles when it is left with the windows down. Leave your car and truck windows rolled up and keep the tent flaps zipped. This will reduce your exposure and hopefully keep your blood level up.

*Popular decal sold at Flamingo resort.*
© 1982, Amelia Bruno, National Park Service.

*Tides can drop dramatically in the Flamingo backcountry, leaving boaters stranded on the mud flats.*
Photo by Martin Smithson.

Captain Hank Brown, a 30-year veteran, and one of the most respected backcountry guides in the Keys, regularly takes charters across the Bay to fish the Flamingo and Cape Sable area. A recent "slight navigation error" resulted in going hard aground amongst the mud and mangroves. On this particular day the wind shifted and prevented the normal rise of backcountry tide which would have allowed them to float off of the mud bar. By dusk, the three anglers were wearing full rain suits and had tissue stuffed in their ears and nostrils to protect them from the mosquitoes and the no-see'ums that had set in like a fog, reducing visibility to six or eight feet.

Having spent an unbearable night in the backcountry, Captain Brown warns that people must be prepared and remember that the salt marsh environment is more severe than you ever imagined. Captain Brown has since purchased a 30 foot extension cable for both his cellular phone antenna and his VHF radio antenna. He can attach the antennas to his 20 foot push pole and gain enough height to "talk to anybody in the world," he says. He now carries extra

*Captain Hank Brown anchors in the East Cape canal and uses live pinfish on a jig for snook near the bottom at slack tide.*
Photo courtesy of Hank Brown.

rain suits, super strength repellent, a mosquito netting hood, flares and various other emergency equipment.

## Fishing

There is plenty of excellent fishing right in the vicinity of Flamingo. Snook, redfish, trout, tarpon and snapper are within easy reach of even the smallest Jon boat. Shallow draft boats are necessary to expand your fishing territory beyond the channels and into the flats. The flats can be very challenging and even frustrating at times because the wind and tide can virtually dry up an entire bay in a matter of hours. It is not only safer, but many times more productive, to fish the edges of the flats from deeper water. This holds true throughout most of Florida Bay.

The entrance to the Flamingo marina basin often produces snook and redfish. Exiting the channel, heading south, you can turn east between markers #10 and #12 and fish the grass flats which lie between the channel and Joe Kemp Key to the east. This area is good for trout. The best bet to use here are the HOOKUP bucktail jigs, jig heads with live shrimp, or the DOA 3″ or 4″ plastic shrimp.

Just south of Joe Kemp Key are a set of pilings or small channel posts. Turn to the left, or north, and you can follow the Snake Bight Channel. Follow the posts, staying to the side of the post where the wooden arrow is pointing. Traveling up the marked channel will provide opportunities for redfish, snook, tarpon, ladyfish and jacks. Look for finger channels that branch off of the main channel and fish these cuts and along the edges. The back end of Snake Bight is a good place to pole the mud flats and look for tailing redfish. Fish the low incoming tide in this area so that you can get back out. Beware of shifting winds out of the north or northeast which can blow the water out of the bight and leave you stranded for days on the mud.

Slightly south of the entrance to the Snake Bight channel, below Joe Kemp Key, is the entrance to the channel heading east called the Tin Can Channel. This channel takes you past Palm Key and Buoy Key to an area below Rankin Bight, about a seven mile trip. Watch for muddy areas in or near the

*Most of the channels around Flamingo provide great snook action.*
Photo by Steve Morgan.

45

Steve Morgan puts Terry Bauer into position for some schooling trout off the East Cape beach.
Photo by Martin Smithson.

The first time we fished this area was really by accident. We were on our way to the East Cape Canal in two boats. Our friends had a warning alarm go off on their outboard motor. While trying to figure out the problem, we drifted along about a half mile off the beach. I spotted two seagulls fluttering around and picking at something on the surface. My son and I cast jigs into the vicinity of these birds and caught trout and jacks on every cast. By the time our friends had the motor problem figured out, we were fished out.

channel which are being churned up by mullet or other fish. These are good spots to try for redfish and trout, especially about halfway between Palm and Buoy Keys. Just east of Buoy Key the area gets deeper—about 3–4 feet. Look for mullet muds in this area which usually indicate trout, snapper and ladyfish present, too.

Another couple of miles east you will find the Dump Keys. The Dump Keys lie southeast of Rankin Key where two passes are marked by stakes. Look for snook and redfish in the area around the passes. The deeper area east of the Dump Keys is considered to be excellent for some of the larger Florida Bay trout.

The flats just west of the Flamingo entrance are productive for trout and redfish especially in the spring and summer on incoming tides. Approximately five miles to the west, about halfway to East Cape, is an area good for spotted seatrout.

Immediately south of the Middle Ground area is the Sandy Key basin and Sandy Key. This is a well known area for summer tarpon. The markers south of Sandy Key can provide some good snapper fishing areas.

The East Cape beaches provide a beautiful backdrop from the water. Not only is the scenery good along these beaches but the fishing can be spectacular, especially for tarpon and snook cruising the shores. This area is well worth exploring.

## Navigating Islamorada to Flamingo Route

The best advice for mastering this route is to hire a guide. They have spent many hours running the various routes and know every discreet marker and short cut. If you think

*Many of the navigable channels are marked with arrows pointing to the deeper water.*

Photo by Martin Smithson.

marked Iron Pipe Channel. Once you've passed through the bank, head North/ Northwest 330° a short distance to the Man of War Channel. This channel will take you North where you then head 342° to the Clive Key Channel. Markers will locate the channel, north to Murray Key which is just south of Flamingo.

The route just described covers a lot of open water and is not well protected. Watch the weather carefully if traveling this way. When there is a moderate chop the guides will typically follow along the lee side of the banks which offer some protection. This technique becomes easier after much experience and familiarity with the route.

that you will make this trip often, go with a guide a few times and study the charts and the aerial photographs and get familiar with the territory. Waterproof Charts® makes a nice map (#33E Florida Bay) which includes the marked channels and the popular routes with compass headings. This would be a good supplemental chart to the aerial photos contained in this book.

There are several routes which the guides take from Islamorada to Flamingo. Their decision is usually based upon the direction of the wind and the amount of chop on the water. The most direct route can be the roughest if the weather is bad. The direct route can be described as: beginning on the northeast side of Peterson Key Bank head northwest about 310° to the marked channel just east of Barnes Key. This channel will get you through the Twin Key Bank. Once through the marked channel, continue on the same heading (310°) to the marked Rabbit Key pass. This channel will turn to the west/southwest and put you in the Rabbit Key Basin. From this point, head west/northwest 294° across the basin to the

Another route from Islamorada to Flamingo is more protected and is often taken during rough weather. This route takes a more northerly course to the Pollock Keys and continues north along the eastern side of the Buttonwood Keys. Just north of the Twisty Mile Channel the route turns west heading through the Dump Keys and on to the Tin Can Channel which leads to Flamingo. This route takes you over some very shallow basins and shoals. While it offers more protection from the wind it is not for the timid boater. 'Tis better to hire a guide, relax and enjoy the beautiful scenery.

# Personal Notes

# Bonefish
## (Albula vulpes)

**Description:**
silvery color with bluish or greenish back, slender; round body; snout long, conical, aiming downward and overhanging lower jaw; dark streaks between scales on upper half of body and faint crossbands extending down to lateral line; extremities of dorsal and caudal fins shaded with black.

**Where found:** primarily inshore fish inhabiting shallows, often less than 1 foot deep, usually over lush grass flats, sand flats and mangrove lagoons. Bonefish range from the Bahamas and Bermuda to southern Brazil, including the Florida Keys; worldwide in tropical waters.

**Size:** 3 to 5 pounds. Florida record: 15 lbs., 6 oz.

**Remarks:** Important sport fish, often occurring in loose schools, except large individuals, which are solitary. Bottom-feeders on shrimp, crabs, worms and small fish. Fish grub for food on the bottom leaving puffs of murky water and muddy trails; their tails may break the surface as they feed.

Bonefish are one of the most sought after fish on the tropical flats. They are said to be warier than a trout and faster than a bullet, giving them the name "ghost of the flats." They provide just enough challenge to catch and display breath-taking lightning runs when hooked, that many of the world's leading anglers rank the bonefish as one of their favorite sport fish.

*Joy Brown, guided by husband Capt. Hank Brown, is all smiles after landing this giant bonefish on fly near Twin Keys.*
Photo by Hank Brown.

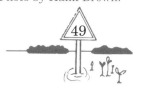

49

From Biscayne Bay, the upper limit of their range, through Key Largo, Islamorada, and Marathon, bonefishing is excellent. Many fish are caught on the oceanside flats and the flats just inside the bay. Some fish are caught as far into the bay as Ninemile Bank. Very few bonefish are caught in the area around Flamingo.

Since bonefish spend most of their time prowling the flats searching for shrimp, crabs, mollusks and small fish, in one to three feet of water, excellent opportunities are provided for the boatless. Wade fishing for bones is an exciting and rewarding technique. The oceanside flats typically have a firm bottom throughout the Keys and are easily accessible from many of the private resorts. Many anglers select their hotels just for that reason.

Tides play an important role in trying to figure out where bonefish will be at a given time. There are plenty of "rules of thumb" and guidelines to follow in the art and science of bonefishing. A basic rule is to fish the first incoming tide as bonefish move up on the flat and are hungry. This is a good basic approach to begin with. However, there can be so many deviations from the norm when dealing with bonefish that it's wise to start with the first incoming tide and fish the complete tidal cycle. For example, at high tide, bonefish can be found along the shoreline edge, especially next to mangroves, and willing to eat.

Bonefish react to many variables other than tide that are constantly changing. The time of year, water temperature, type of flat, availability of food, direction of current, all affect where the bonefish feed and travel. It's like the old question "when is the best time to fish for bonefish?" My favorite response is "when you can find time."

## Catching Bonefish

There are several ways to catch a bonefish, some more sporting than others.

Light spinning tackle in the six, eight or ten pound class is most common. Using four pound test on ultra-light would be very sporting. The most common bait is live shrimp. Next would be a shrimp and a jig combo, a shrimp tipped jig, a plain bucktail jig and then a fly, in the ascending order of "sportiness." However, this doesn't always mean that a shrimp is a sure bet over a well placed fly. Sometimes the sudden plop of a cast shrimp will spook the fish, sending them on their way.

My brother-in-law and my son each caught their first bonefish in the Keys on a quarter ounce HOOKUP, white, bucktail jig. The jig has a small grizzly hackle feather which makes it look very much like a hand-tied fly. Their fish were caught in two feet of water from a boat, poling along the edge of a flat. Captain Hank Brown, maker of the jig, says that in two feet of water, or deeper, the jigs are very effective. Once you get into more shallow conditions, you should switch to shrimp or fly. Bonefish tend to spook more easily in shallow water.

Live shrimp can provide a lot of bonefish action if fishing the deeper edges of flats or around cuts or

*Rob Smithson caught his first bonefish on a white jig near Teatable Key.*
Photo by Martin Smithson.

channels. A HOOKUP jig and shrimp combo is the best bet. Pinch the fantail off of the shrimp so that the shrimp will not spin when retrieved. Run the hook through the tail, starting at the bottom side of the shrimp and exiting out the topside. This will allow you to twitch the shrimp backwards imitating a fleeing shrimp.

When using shrimp in shallow grass flats it is best to use a bare #2 to 1/0 hook. Again pinch the tail off, but this time thread the shrimp onto the hook and exit midway, out of the belly. Gently pull the hook and line through the shrimp's body until the eye of the hook, and line, are all that remains in the shrimp. Now rotate the hook upwards so that you can push the hook point up into the shrimp's body, burying the point just under the top shell of the shrimp. This completely hides the hook and makes it weedless. This is a great rig for teasing bonefish when you are wading in shallow, grassy areas.

Commander John Moore, USN Ret., of Cocoa Beach, Florida is one of the state's more colorful characters with an adventuresome background as a Naval combat pilot, aviation test pilot, manager of the Apollo test operations and previous mayor of Cocoa Beach. After retiring over 20 years ago with a continuing thirst for adventure, he chose to make regular trips to Islamorada in search of bonefish.

Mr. Moore shared with me some wonderful stories and his bonefishing technique. He enjoyed most, telling about the three-day weekend when President George Bush hit a dry spell and didn't catch a bonefish. Mr. Moore and his friend managed to hook 27 bonefish and land 17 of them during the same three days.

His technique is very relaxed and more of a family style way of fishing. He likes to anchor near the drop-off of a flat, anchoring in shallow water and casting into three to five feet of water off the drop, especially during an incoming tide. He uses 10 pound test, a #1 hook and live shrimp, hooked through the tail. However, he uses six outfits, keeping six lines in the water. With cold beverages on hand, he says it's just a waiting game.

His favorite spots are: off the tip of Tea Table Key, where he caught his first bonefish, the shoal just south of Cowpens Cut, the edges of Cross Bank, the oceanside of Snake Creek and the north side of Shell Key.

The great challenge in bonefishing is to put a bait or lure where the fish can see it without being spooked. This is difficult since bonefish are constantly on the move and seem to change direction every ten feet. This is where fly fishing provides a slight advantage allowing for a quiet presentation of the fly. Fly casting also allows for several presentations to the same fish.

The typical size fly is on a #2 hook for shallow flats, one foot or less. As the depth increases, to two or three feet, the size of the fly can increase up to a 1/0 hook. Bonefish flies have weighted eyes so they will sink quickly, giving them a jig effect. Short strips will give the appearance of a small shrimp diving for cover.

Even when fly fishing, many guides will stake out near a popular bonefish flat and throw pieces of fresh shrimp into an open sand area. This chumming effect will attract bonefish into plain view giving the fly caster some good targets.

## Releasing Bonefish

Catching a bonefish is purely for sport. They are not considered a food fish and should not be kept. If you want a mounted fish for your wall at office or home, all you need is a photograph and measurements (length and girth) of the released fish. Plastic replicas are easily obtained from a taxidermist.

The allure of the bonefish is intense as it is indeed a glamorous fish. Sportsmen and women around the world will spend hundreds, if not thousands of dollars to capture their prize fish. It is understandable that many will want to document their catch with a photograph, for long term bragging rights, and justification of an invested fortune. Here are some tips to consider when photographing and releasing bonefish:

Bonefish are relatively easy and safe to handle with bare hands. You can grasp them at the base of the tail and by the lower lip. Do not run your fingers down their throat as they have crushers which could turn the end of your thumb into crab pulp. Keep the fish wet. Have your pose already thought out and the cameras ready before removing the fish from the water.

Take the pictures quickly. Gently hold the fish and slightly rotate the dorsal fin (topside) toward the camera. The side of a bonefish, if held flat to the camera, can reflect light like a bright mirror and ruin the photo, especially if using a fill flash. Work quickly and return the fish to the water within one minute or less. Sixty seconds is a long time. Try running a hundred yard dash a couple of times and then hold your breath under water for a minute to see what it must feel like to the fish.

When releasing the fish, hold it by the base of its tail and move it back and forth under water to get water moving through its mouth and across the gills. It will need time to absorb oxygen from the water, diffusing across the gills and into the blood which feeds the muscles. When the fish struggles to get away it is usually safe to let it go.

If the fish has been severely stressed it may swim upright for a few feet then cartwheel and turn belly up. If this happens, grab the fish and continue working it back and

*The sides of a bonefish can reflect light like a glass mirror.*
Photo by Martin Smithson.

forth to get more oxygen exchange in the water. This may take some time. I have worked with fish for 15 to 20 minutes before they regained the necessary strength to vigorously swim away. If a disoriented fish is left to fend for itself, it will die or be eaten by a shark.

Be sure and give the bonefish the same amount of respect that you expect to receive when others admire your photo.

### Preferred Bonefish Fly Patterns

**Crazy Charlie** = classic bonefish fly
**Clouser Minnow** = for deeper flats
**Gotcha** = common Bahamian pattern
A good rule is to match the fly with the color of the flat-white or tan for sandy flats, brown and olive over turtle grass. When stripping use 3" to 6" erratic jerks and pulses to imitate a fleeing shrimp. If a bonefish follows, speed up with longer strips (retrieve) and frequent pauses. If sudden resistance is felt when the bonefish pins the fly to the bottom, continue with very short retrieves until the fish sucks the fly into its mouth. Then use a longer stroke or "slip strike" to set the hook. Never sweep the rod to the side and risk pulling the fly away from the fish. This takes great willpower.

# Tarpon
## (Megalops atlanticus)

**Description:**
last ray of dorsal fin extended into long filament; one dorsal fin; back dark blue to green or greenish black, shading into bright silver on the sides; may be brownish gold in estuarine waters; huge scales; mouth large and points upward.

Similar species: (as juveniles) ladyfish, *Elops saurus*.

Where found: primarily inshore fish, although adult fish spawn offshore where the ribbon-like larval stage of the fish can be found. Tarpon range from Virginia, Bermuda, and Gulf of Mexico to Brazil.

Size: Most catches average 40 to 50 pounds

Florida record: 243 lbs.

Remarks: slow grower; matures at 7 to 13 years of age; spawning occurs between May and September; females may lay more than 12 million eggs; can tolerate wide range of salinity; juveniles commonly found in fresh water; can breathe air at the surface; feeds mainly on fish and large crustaceans.

A primitive animal with more than 300 million years of ancestry, the tarpon is the most exciting gamefish in the Keys.

With its huge scales and an upward turned mouth for gulping air, resembling the ancient lungfish, tarpon reign as the silver king with modern light tackle fishermen.

When tarpon are hooked, they don't just jump, they erupt with powerful fury, shaking and crashing as if the magnificent beast knows that its life depends on being able to spit the hook out. More often than not, the tarpon wins this incredibly brief, desperate battle for life. The resulting adrenaline surge for the angler is what attracts legions of tarpon hunters to the Keys and Florida Bay.

*Randy Towe fights a leaping tarpon in Florida Bay.*
Courtesy of Papa Joe's Marina.

Tarpon were once thought to live about 20 years. We now know that they live much longer. The oldest tarpon caught off Florida's east coast weighed 238 pounds and was determined to be 55 years old.

Another tarpon caught off the Florida Keys in 1935 provides living proof of a tarpon's longevity. This fish is still alive today, residing in a Chicago aquarium, and is over 60 years old!

53

On the average, tarpon live between 15 and 40 years and are very slow growing. They are 8 to 10 years old and weigh 40 to 50 pounds before they reach sexual maturity. Males never get over 80 pounds so most of those huge trophy mounts seen decorating the walls of restaurants and fish houses are, or were, females. Adult tarpon spend the winter offshore in the deep blue. In May and June they move inshore to feed. Many tarpon anglers fishing the passes in the Keys in June think that the fish are coming in to spawn. The fact is that their sex organs are not yet at a stage to allow spawning. The tarpon are there strictly to feed. Their diet is almost entirely made up of crabs. One large tarpon's stomach was found to contain enough crabs to fill a 5 gallon bucket. By July the female tarpon are full of roe. One female will carry over 20 million eggs and the roe may weigh 15 pounds. The eggs begin to swell and the tarpon begin to form big schools just off the beaches. They form the classic large daisy chain and then move offshore to spawn.

*If you want to see wild tarpon, up close, visit the dock at Robbie's Boat Rentals, mile marker 77.5, located on the bayside at the lower end of Lignumvitae bridge. These fish started hanging around almost 20 years ago, looking for handouts.* Photo by Martin Smithson.

In the mid 1970's, before anglers were required to purchase a $50 permit to kill one tarpon annually, hundreds of tarpon were killed in Florida for mounts. One taxidermist in the Keys was mounting 500 tarpon per year. With today's restrictions and the advent of plastic mounts, only 100 tarpon were killed in 1992. Most tarpon angling today is a catch and release sport.

Tarpon season in the Keys is considered to be April, May and June when they are most abundant. However, tarpon are caught year 'round. There are different types of tarpon fishing to select from in the Keys: Poling the edges of flats, staking out along popular migration routes, fishing channels and fishing the bridges. Tarpon fishing around the bridges is discussed in the chapter on "Shallow Water Fishing Techniques."

It is surprising to many that such a large gamefish can be pursued on such light tackle. Many anglers will use 10 to 20 lb. test line with a 30 to 40 lb. test monofilament shock leader. When using light tackle, the sharpness of the hook becomes a critical factor. Tarpon have a hard bony mouth that makes initial hook penetration difficult, not to mention what happens after hook penetration is attempted. The explosive head shaking routine also complicates a good hook set. Therefore, use sharp, sharp hooks. Many guides now believe that it's best to flatten the barb for easier penetration, and play the fish properly to keep the fish from throwing the hook.

Because of the variety of ways to approach tarpon it is advised to hire a guide who is familiar with their patterns and can greatly increase your odds of hooking up. If you do decide to fish on your own, talk with the local tackle shops and some of the guides at the marinas. Find out if the oceanside flats, bayside flats or the channels are your best bet.

Tarpon have the potential to eat just about anything so don't worry about a super specialized selection of tackle. They will take jigs, jig and shrimp, plugs, the D.O.A. shrimp and D.O.A.. Terroreyz and most live baits. Tarpon will eat mullet, pinfish, pilchards, crabs, trout, ladyfish and even catfish. Tarpon will even feast on dead bait. I have seen tarpon take mullet heads and have heard stories of giant tarpon engulfing a small dolphin carcass at a marina.

Live bait is undoubtedly the most popular tarpon offering and should be rigged with a super sharp 2/0 to 5/0 hook. In the spring and summer of the year when you are likely to encounter 100 pound plus fish, use the larger hooks and heavier tackle. In the late summer and fall, scale back to smaller hooks and lighter tackle because the average

*With a mouth that opens like a cargo transport, tarpon still don't hesitate to eat a small fly.*
Courtesy of Hank Brown.

tarpon is going to be closer to 30 lbs. When using bait, fish the channels and deeper areas just off the flats and banks. Use a float three to four feet above the bait. Tarpon eyes are always looking up and will blast the bait from underneath. Use the aerials in this book to locate the popular tarpon spots.

What is exciting about fishing in the Keys is that you frequently encounter the unexpected. While fishing with companions out of three different flats boats we were poling the shallow flats around the Peterson Keys hoping to scare up some bonefish. Brian Lightle of Melbourne, Florida was armed with a live shrimp on a #1 hook on 10 lb. test line with no leader. I heard Brian yell across the water, "Look at that wake coming towards us." Brian cast his small shrimp in front of the wake and all hell broke loose. For the next ten minutes Brian and Captain Don Perchalski chased a 100 lb. plus tarpon across the bay only to be ended by one spectacular jump. Ten minutes on light line with no leader was more than anyone expected.

*Using live bait under a float is most effective for tarpon.*
Courtesy of Hank Brown.

Whether on fly or spin, tarpon fishing demands that a great deal more attention be paid to the equipment, i.e. drag setting, knots, hooks, than for most species. Second to the importance of equipment is the fighting technique with tarpon. When the great mass of a tarpon's body goes airborne, you must bow to the fish by thrusting your rod tip towards the jumping fish. This throws slack in the line and reduces the chance of breaking the line or the hook being thrown out.

Stu Apte of Islamorada is well known for his tarpon tactics and fighting techniques that he perfected as a guide in the 1960's. His knowledge of the tarpon is still very accurate today so it would be worthwhile to read "Stu Apte's Fishing in the Florida Keys and Flamingo." Originally published in 1976, this book can be purchased at H.T. Chittum and Co. in Islamorada. Apte is also credited with the development of the Keys style tarpon streamer. While these flies were tied on 3/0 and 5/0 hooks in the early tarpon days, today the same style is used, but tied on much smaller hooks. Even though this is a specialized fly, tarpon will eat most any fly designed for saltwater species. Once you hook a tarpon on the fly rod, you might as well chalk up another addiction.

# Permit
## (*Trachinotus falcatus*)

Description: color gray, dark or iridescent blue above, shading to silvery sides, in dark waters showing golden tints around breast; small permit have teeth on tongue (none on pompano); dorsal fin insertion directly above that of the anal fin; 17 to 21 soft dorsal rays; 16 to 19 soft anal rays.

Similar fish: pompano, *T. carolinus*. The permit is deeper bodied; pompano rarely grow larger than 6 pounds; permit common to 40 pounds.

Where found: offshore on wrecks and debris, inshore on grass flats, sand flats, and in channels; most abundant in south Florida, with smaller specimens from every coastal county. Permit range from Massachusetts to southeast Brazil, including the Bahamas and in the West Indies.

Size: common to 25 pounds

Florida record: 51 lbs., 8 oz.

Remarks: feeds mainly on bottom-dwelling crabs, shrimp, small clams, and small fish.

Permit are one of those prized and highly respected fish in the Keys that are seen more often than they are caught. Some of the most experienced anglers in Florida have yet to catch a permit. Bonefish experts refer to permit as the bonefish's heavyweight brother. Permit share similar habits with the bonefish in the way they feed, tail, frequent similar areas, skittishness and their powerful, drag smoking runs when hooked.

Permit are present in the Keys all year but are more plentiful in the spring throughout the fall. May seems to be the best month. In

*Ty Pico displays a trophy permit he caught while guided by Steve Thomas.*
Courtesy of Papa Joe's Marina.

June permit concentrate in deep water where they are thought to be spawning. In August they return to the flats until cold weather drives them back to deep water.

Permit require deeper water than bonefish because of their deep body profile. They prefer hard coral bottom where they patrol along the outside edges of oceanside flats in two to five feet of water.

57

Some flats offer these conditions around the outer edges of Florida Bay where hard bottom flats adjoin deep channels. Permit are encountered in the upper Keys, however, their numbers increase significantly in the middle Keys to the flats between Key West and the Marquesas. They also frequent bridge channels such as the Indian Key Bridge which has become well known for the permit.

The most popular bait for permit is a small live crab, about the size of a silver dollar, on a 2/0 hook. Fifteen pound test tackle is fine but make sure the spool has plenty of capacity. A permit can rip off 300 yards of line in a hurry.

Permit are occasionally caught on jigs and even plastic grubs or worms. However, artificials account for a significantly smaller number of fish than live bait. Catching a permit on fly has been called the supreme angling challenge. If your mission is to catch a permit on the fly, or otherwise, it is highly recommended that you hire a guide who specializes in the pursuit of permit.

To quote Mark Sosin and Lefty Kreh, from their book "Fishing the Flats," "Maddening elusiveness is what permit fishing is all about."

*Carin Beaulieu of Sportfishing Magazine and Capt. Bruce Stagg with a double header caught and released during a Redbone Media Tournament.* Courtesy of Papa Joe's Marina.

Permit spook easier than a bonefish. If one fish in a school becomes skittish, they all disappear together. Bait should be cast low to the water with the rod tip raised just before the bait lands. This will give it a skittering action that imitates a fleeing crab or shrimp and often draws a strike from the permit. Live shrimp is the second most popular bait and should be cast the same way.

# Snook
## (Centropomus undecimalis)

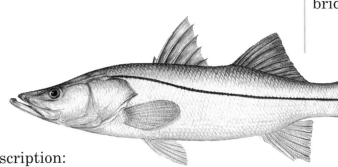

Description:
distinct black lateral line; high, divided dorsal fin; sloping forehead; large mouth, protruding lower jaw; grows much larger than other snooks; pelvic fin yellow.

Similar fish:  other Centropomus, e.g. fat snook, swordspine snook

Where found: from central Florida south to southern Brazil, usually inshore in coastal and brackish waters, along mangrove shorelines, seawalls, and bridges; also on reefs and pilings nearshore.

Size:  most catches 5 to 8 pounds

Florida record:  44 lbs., 3 ozs.

Remarks:  spawns primarily in summer; cannot tolerate water temperatures below 60°F; can tolerate wholly fresh or saltwater; schools along shore and in passes during spawning season; feeds on fish and larger crustaceans.

If the distribution of snook was not restricted to the warm waters of the southern half of Florida, then surely snook anglers would outnumber bass anglers in this country.

Snook share some of the same habits as the popular freshwater black bass. However, when comparing fight per pound, the snook offers some of the most heart stopping, surging, thrashing action in their desperate retreat to cover after being hooked. Most snook successfully make it to the cover they seek such as mangrove roots, dock pilings or bridge abutments.

The common snook has some interesting biological characteristics which aren't so common. Snook may exhibit hermaphroditism, or male-to-female sex reversal as they grow older. Thus, most younger and smaller adults are males and most older, larger adults are females. Sex reversal is a reproductive adaptation which insures the species' success.

Environmental conditions may stimulate sex reversal, especially when times get tough. This keeps entire populations from being wiped out due to freezes, droughts, or disappearance of their primary food source.

Snook are very sensitive to cool water temperatures. At 60 degrees fahrenheit they become sluggish and at water temperatures near 50 degrees they die. Temperature is the factor which limits their range in Florida. In severe winters, even in south Florida, there may be a high mortality rate when water temperature drops suddenly.

Snook are considered an inshore saltwater fish, however, they may be found in salt or fresh water. They are tolerant of wide ranges of salinity, frequently migrating significant distances up freshwater tributaries which feed into Florida Bay. Snook have a strong preference for mangrove shorelines and are also known to be fond of moving water.

The most common size snook caught by anglers is in the three to five pound range. Fish exceeding 50 pounds have been taken in Florida but no one has been able to break the long standing conventional tackle record recognized by the

International Game Fish Association of Pompano Beach. That record is a 53 pound 10 ounce snook caught off Costa Rica in 1978.

Most snook, males and females, are sexually mature and ready to reproduce by the time they reach 24 inches in length. Some snook become sexually mature as small as 13 inches.

The peak spawning season for snook is June and July, with some spawning as late as October. Spawning activity seems to be associated with new and/or full moon phases.

A mature female can shed more than one-and-a-half million eggs. Snook require salty water to produce viable sperm and buoyant eggs. Therefore the snook spawn near the ocean passes and just offshore.

The snook's main diet is fish. During a day of feeding, the bulk of the stomach's weight will be from fish like the finger mullet and pinfish. Shrimp and crabs will outnumber the consumed fish but do not represent as much weight. It appears that snook will not hesitate to take a number of small tasty snacks, whenever available.

For those anglers who frequently catch snook and worry about the survival of their releases, results from a recent study should put their minds at ease. Several thousand snook have been studied in Florida to evaluate the success of catch and release. Conclusions from these studies indicate that mortality of snook caught on hook-and-line and released is extremely low. The only deaths that occur are when fish are "gut hooked", as a result of swallowing the bait or lure. When snook are hooked in the lips using artificial lures, one hundred percent survival is documented.

*Rob Smithson has become known as the "Snook Slayer" in our family. His speciality is soft plastic jigs and jerk baits.*
Photo by Martin Smithson.

Most snook in the Keys are caught around bridges or from mid-Florida Bay in potholes, to the southern Everglades in small channels and cuts. Most are taken on live bait-fish, live shrimp, jigs, plugs and flies.

Fishing for snook around the bridges is discussed in the chapter on Shallow Water Fishing Techniques. Snook fishing at night from bridges is all but a religion for many local anglers.

Backcountry snook fishing starts several miles into the bay where the

fish are either found in deeper pockets next to small mangrove islands or lying in potholes on the flats. Potholes are slight depressions in the bay bottom which are one to two feet deeper than the surrounding flat.

It is interesting how potholes form in the bay. Most potholes, which vary from a few feet in diameter to 20 feet or more, are actually small sinkholes. The base of Florida Bay consists of built-up limestone deposits. Occasionally pockets of limestone under the bay bottom dissolve over time causing the bottom to subside or sink, creating the pothole. This slightly deeper depression is a real attraction for snook, and provides a place to rest, to get out of the current, especially on an outgoing tide.

Snook also use the holes as ambush points where they can go undetected until an unsuspecting pinfish, needlefish, mullet or

Liz Levenson hoists a backcountry snook caught near Flamingo with Captain Hank Brown.
Courtesy of Hank Brown.

shrimp passes by. This is where a well placed bucktail jig, plug or fly will entice the "ole sneaky snook."

Spotting the holes is not difficult, provided the water is relatively clear. The holes are lighter in color compared to the darker turtlegrass and brown vegetation. Once you spot one, you should find several more in the same vicinity. Do not pole over the hole but maneuver within casting distance. Pay attention to the direction of moving water. The bait, or food sources, that the snook is waiting for drift over the hole with the current. Therefore, cast your lure just up current of the hole so that it will be presented to the snook in a natural manner. Of course it is more exciting to see the snook lying in a hole before you make the perfect cast. However, most of the time you will be blind casting to the potholes as the snook can be very difficult to see. With this in mind, do not hesitate to cast to every hole.

Other popular snook hangouts (marked on the aerial photos) are the deeper cuts through shallow banks and around small islands, especially near the Flamingo area. The canals near Flamingo, including the East Cape Canal which leads to backcountry creeks around Lake Ingraham, hold plenty of snook. A surefire technique for these areas is to stake out or anchor near deep water which cuts under overhanging mangroves. Toss a 1/4 oz. HOOKUP jig with a live shrimp close to the trees and hang on.

An important reminder when snook fishing: snook have a mouth full of sandpaper-like patches for teeth that can chafe right through monofilament line just above the hook. If that doesn't work, they have a razor sharp gill plate that when flared out during battle will cut through line like a knife through butter. Be sure to use at least 25 to 30 lb. test leader for snook. Also be careful of the gill plate when handling.

How to bait hook for
Bone fish — P. 51

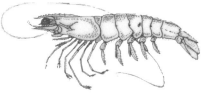

# Spotted Seatrout
## (Cynoscion nebulosus)

Description: dark gray or green above, with sky-blue tinges shading to silvery and white below, numerous distinct round black spots on back, extending to the dorsal fins and tail; black margin on posterior of tail; no barbells; no scales on the soft dorsal fin; one or two prominent canine teeth usually present at tip of upper jaw.

Similar fish: other seatrout

Where found: inshore and/or nearshore over grass, sand, and sandy mud bottoms; move into slow-moving or still, deep waters in cold weather. Seatrout range from New York to southern Florida and the entire Gulf of Mexico.

Size: common to 4 pounds on west coast and Florida Bay, larger on east coast.

Florida record: The Florida record, just over 17 pounds, caught near Fort Pierce Inlet is also a world record.

Remarks: matures during first or second year and spawn inshore from March through November; often in association with seagrass beds; lives mainly in estuaries and moves only short distances; adults feed mainly on shrimp and small fish; prefers water temperatures between 58 to 81°F, and may be killed if trapped in shallow water during cold weather, longevity 8 to 10 years.

Ask Florida fishermen to list their favorite fish, and the majority will place spotted seatrout right at the top.

For years, the seatrout has ranked as the most desirable sport species of Florida inshore waters and it continues to be one of the top commercially sought fish in the state.

The spotted seatrout is a prolific spawner. The older the female, the more eggs are produced. A 4-year-old female trout, for example, will produce 15,000 eggs while a 6-year-old will produce 150,000 eggs. And, as remarkable as it might sound, an 8-year-old female can produce over a million eggs.

*John Wehle, a regular visitor in the Keys, enjoys all Florida Bay species, especially big trout.*
Photo by Martin Smithson.

It becomes obvious why current fishing regulations only allow the possession of one trout over 20 inches in length. The 7 and 8-year-old breeder trout, which are typically over the 24 inch mark, need to be left in the population to ensure the species' success.

It appears that trout don't spawn on the shallow grass flats as many fishermen believe. Instead, the trout seek out deeper channels and holes with sand or mud bottoms which are adjacent to vegetated flats.

*Captain Paul Glanville points out a trout mud in Florida Bay.*
Photo by Martin Smithson.

Several males gather in a vicinity and start drumming. The drumming activity only seems to occur at certain times, between two hours after dark and midnight. Within 24 hours, free-floating fertilized eggs are found after being released by the attracted females.

After a couple of days, the eggs hatch and the young drift in the water for four to seven days, before scattering to the seagrass beds where they hide for six to eight weeks.

After this tender period they start to school and continue to exhibit schooling behavior until they are five years of age. By this time, most of the males have died and the females become solitary.

Of the average trout diet, 85 percent consists of other fish such as mullet, pinfish and needlefish. Only 15 percent of their diet is made up of shrimp and crabs.

Seatrout capture their prey by lunging and grasping the prey with their prominent canine teeth. They are capable of ingesting fish up to a third of the length of their own body.

Trout are found in the Florida Bay, from a few miles north of the main Keys to Flamingo. The most popular method of finding trout in the bay is to look for mullet muds. These are noticeable areas where the bottom has been churned up, turning the water murky. It may be a small area, the size of a small room, or take up an entire cove. As the mullet feed on plankton, algae and small worms on the bottom, larger animals such as shrimp and small fish scurry out of the way. Trout and other fish come to join in on the feast. The trout themselves will continue to keep the bottom stirred up.

*The Donnmar pliers are handy for mashing down barbs, when schooling trout require quick releases, without injury to the fish.*
Photo by Martin Smithson.

Once you find the trout, there are a variety of ways to catch them. Many soft artificial baits such as the D.O.A. Shrimp and Terroreyz, and grub tail jigs are very productive. The advantage of using artificials is that many casts are made, covering a wider area where there might be fish. Artificials work very well in slightly cloudy water. If the water is clear, live bait will have the advantage.

The most popular trout catching technique in the bay is the combination of live shrimp and a popping cork. The cone-shaped popping cork, found in virtually all tackle shops, keeps the live bait suspended at the right depth, and makes an intriguing sound to the trout. A sudden jerk on the line and cork creates a "ploop" sound that is similar to the sound trout make when hitting topwater. The best technique is to pop the cork about once every 30 seconds. Popping too frequently makes the trout suspicious.

*Mathew DelToro caught this beauty on a bucktail jig in a north Florida Bay bight.*
Photo by Hank Brown.

A compromise technique between live bait and artificials is the use of small shrimp pieces (fresh or frozen) to tip a bucktail or grub tail jig. The added scent is too much temptation for a timid trout. This is also a great way to locate trout when drifting across a grass flat which is known to produce trout. Blind casting, casting into general areas before you have actually seen a fish, covers a lot of territory and will often help you identify the zone (depth and location) where the trout are hanging out.

Spotted seatrout is a wonderful species to get acquainted with fly fishing. My son and I used to use the jig and shrimp method described above to locate schools of trout. We would then put away the spinning rods and pick up the fly rods (7 wt. and 8 wt.) and throw clouser minnow patterns. My favorite is a tan and white with a little flash. It was a delight to finally see my son catching fish on fly. For anyone who has taken up fly fishing and has run into a frustrating dry spell, the seatrout can be very accommodating and bring instant relief.

Topwater trout action is amazing and entertaining. Some trout will get so aggressive and excited over a topwater lure, that they will come completely out of the water. I have seen small trout bust a floating plug and turn a flip in the process. On fly, small foam or deer-hair poppers will bring on some exciting topwater action. On spinning tackle, plugs like Heddon's Zara Spook, Zara Puppy and Baby Torpedo, Mirr-O-Lures, Bang-O-Lure and the Jumping Minnow will generate some action. Larger fish are wise and wary. The best fish will most likely be taken on the longer casts from the boat, which the heavier plugs allow for.

# Personal Notes

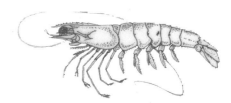

# Redfish (red drum)
## *(Sciaenops ocellatus)*

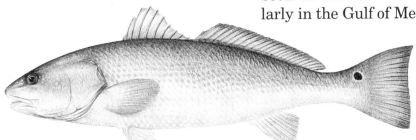

Description: chin without barbells; copper-bronze body, lighter shade in clear water; one to many spots at base of tail (rarely no spots); mouth horizontal and opening downward; scales large.

Similar fish: Black drum, *Pogonias cromis*.

Where found: juveniles are an inshore fish, migrating out of the estuaries at about 30 inches (4 years) and joining the spawning population offshore. Redfish range from Massachusetts to northern Mexico, including south Florida.

Size: one of 27 inches weighs about 8 pounds

Florida record: 51 lbs., 8 ozs.

Remarks: spawning occurs from August to November in nearshore waters; sudden cold snaps may kill red drum in shallow inshore waters; feeds on crustaceans, fish, and mollusks; longevity to 20 years or more.

Except for bonefish in the tropics, no other species of fish has brought so much attention to flats fishing, especially in Florida, than the redfish. And it has happened in only the past few years.

The redfish (red drum) fishery does have quite a long history. As early as the 1700's, a substantial sport and commercial fishery existed from Virginia southward to Georgia. Recreational and commercial fishermen had been in conflict since prior to 1900, particularly in the Gulf of Mexico. Over eighty years of wide-open commercial netting and sportfishing without bag limits decimated the redfish populations in most parts of its range.

In the early to mid 1980's, estimated recreational landings were as high as commercial landings (approximately 1 million pounds) and even higher in 1985. Then entered the "blackened redfish" restaurant craze.

In the first six months of 1986, the commercial harvest of red drum in the Gulf of Mexico exceeded five million pounds. The National Marine Fisheries Service responded with a three-month moratorium. By the late '80's state and federal commissions had implemented increased size limits and closed seasons for the sport fishermen and a total shutdown of the offshore purse seining and inshore commercial netting.

*Redfish are built for grubbing on the bottom.*
Photo by Martin Smithson.

Following these restrictions, the recovery of the redfish stocks has been measurable. As a result of strict harvest regulations, "redfish on the flats" is a very popular and growing sport in Florida Bay.

In shallow waters the redfish "tail" much like bonefish and provide a good target for sight fishing. Redfish are mainly bottom feeders and will show the tip of their bluish tail when they tip up to grab a crab on the bay bottom. They spend a lot of time grubbing along the bottom and will stay in the general feeding vicinity for a number of days if not disturbed. Adult redfish can grow to over 50 pounds and have been found in schools of over a hundred fish.

Young redfish feed on mysid shrimp, marine insects and worms. As redfish grow older they continue to feed on these items while grubbing on the flats, however, larger penaeid shrimp, crabs and fish become increasingly important in the diet. Favorite prey fish include mullet, spot and pinfish. Several studies suggest that blue crabs may be the most important prey of large adult redfish.

*Dee Thomas, guided by her husband, Capt. Steve Thomas, didn't have to travel far from Papa Joe's to find this redfish.* Courtesy of Papa Joe's Marina.

If you've ever wondered why recreational fishing regulations placed a size slot limit on redfish (not less than 18 inches or more than 27 inches) it is based on the population dynamics of the species. Redfish have an unusually high annual mortality rate for young two year old fish, over 75 percent. Therefore only a small portion of the population survives to reach maturity. This group of relatively small fish, just under 18 inches, needs to be protected.

Redfish don't reach sexual maturity until they are approximately 28 inches long. Thus, the spawning population is protected by limiting harvested fish to no more than 27 inches in length. Then there's the daily bag limit of one fish, which further protects the breeding stock.

In the Keys, redfish don't really start to show until you get six or seven miles north into Florida Bay. From this point you can find redfish all the way to Flamingo and the surrounding backcountry. There are certain areas that are known to regularly produce redfish. In these areas the guides will pole around the flats and look for tailing redfish. Other signs they look for are mud trails. Where some species, like snook, leave puffs of mud when they spook out of an area, redfish leave a muddy trail due to the fact that they run so close to the bottom.

Once the fish are located, they are relatively easy to stalk. Redfish are built for grubbing on the bottom with their blunt head, bottom-slung mouth and turned-down eyes. When tailing, they are so busy rooting the bottom and taking in food by

sucking or biting the bottom, that they hardly notice your presence. A well placed jig, right on their nose, will most always get their attention.

Redfish are so willing to take an artificial that it's really not worth the effort to use live bait for reds. If you feel you must, live shrimp are difficult for a redfish to resist.

You don't always have to sight cast to redfish in shallow water. Many of the islands in the bay are partially surrounded by deeper channels. These areas sometimes hold redfish that are more than ready to jump on a shrimp or a jig. This is called blind casting and is common in deeper water where you can't see the fish, but where you expect they might be.

Jigs are very popular among redfish anglers. The different jig head shapes allows one to fish in a variety of conditions. Butterbean shaped heads sink fast. Something you'll want when fishing the deeper water where flats drop off. The HOOKUP jigs are shaped so that the hook will ride with the point on top, reducing snags and resulting in a quick "hookup." Flat heads similar to the bonefish jigs will skim across shallow grass beds and should be used where reds are tailing. Many of the Florida Bay guides like chartreuse and white bucktail jigs. The soft tailed jigs are also very effective. Most jigs are worked relatively slow for redfish by lifting the rod to create a quick twitch then a hesitation

which lets the jig fall like a wounded baitfish. If the reds aren't cooperating, try tipping the jig with a small piece of shrimp for scent. Sometimes that's all it takes. For versatility you can't beat a box full of jigs for redfish.

Redfish readily eat flies and make excellent targets for the fly rod angler. As stated earlier in the chapter on fishing techniques, Flip Pallot believes that redfish were specifically designed for the "enjoyment of beginning fly fisherfolk."

The fly tackle used for redfish is very similar to what you would use for snook or trout. A seven weight to nine weight outfit with floating line and a section of 20 pound shock or bite tippet is perfect. The most popular flies would have to be a clouser minnow pattern or a seaducer pattern with small weighted eyes. The weighted eyes in both patterns cause the fly to hop up and down when stripped, suggestive of a nervous crustacean or a small wounded bait fish. Again, the popular color is chartreuse. However, many other colors and patterns are effective and should be tried when one seems to be rejected. Consult with a guide and/or the local tackle shop.

Redfish are very tough saltwater fish. They don't need delicate handling but need some care when releasing. Redfish get very tired after a lengthy battle and will die if allowed to sink to the bottom without being rejuvenated. Pump water across the gills by holding the fish by the tail and moving the fish back and forth in the water. This allows oxygen to enter the bloodstream and replenish the tired muscles. In hot weather, warm water does not contain as much oxygen as cooler water. It is difficult to get a redfish rejuvenated in the hot summer. That is why it is important to use heavy enough tackle (8–10 lb.) to bring a fish in, in a short period of time, without completely exhausting the fish. Once a fish begins to swim on it's own, staying upright, you can let it go, knowing that you are perpetuating the sport without depleting the resource.

*Redfish school in shallow bights in North Florida Bay.*
Courtesy of Hank Brown.

# Personal Notes

# Mangrove Snapper
## (*Lutjanus griseus*)

Description: Color dark brown or gray with reddish or orange spots in rows along the sides; dark horizontal band from snout through eye (young only); two conspicuous canine teeth at front of upper jaw; dorsal fins have dark or reddish borders; no dark spot on side underneath dorsal fin.

Similar fish: Cubera snapper, *L. cyanopterus*.

Where found: juveniles inshore in tidal creeks, mangroves, and grass beds; adults generally nearshore or offshore on coral or rocky reefs.

Mangrove snapper, more often referred to as gray snapper outside of Florida, range from Massachusetts, Bermuda and northern Gulf of Mexico to southeast Brazil and eastern Atlantic.

Size: one to three pounds inshore, eight to 10 pounds offshore. Florida record: 16 lbs., 8 ozs.

Remarks: spawns June through August; feeds on crustaceans and small fish. An excellent food fish, sometimes marketed as "Red Snapper."

Mangrove snapper are a staple in the Keys. They are most numerous in the southern half of Florida. In the clear waters of the Keys they can be seen in pods, hanging around bridge pilings, underneath docks and along mangrove shorelines. They are also plentiful over both inner and outer reefs. They are wonderful fish for kids as they strike furiously and give a good fight for their small size. Many Florida anglers can give the snapper credit for their first fish experience when all that was needed was a hook and piece of cut bait, dropped on a line from just about any dock.

While it sounds easy, mangrove snapper can be darn finicky at times, especially the big ones. You may see a horde of fish lurking around a dock piling. Drop a piece of shrimp

*Derek Busby pulled this hungry snapper out from under a mangrove tree.*
Photo by Martin Smithson.

or cut bait and watch it instantly vanish. Drop the same bait with a hook in it and watch fish rush the bait, only to stop an inch short and slowly back up with a suspicious look. The best way to beat them at this game is to chum with broken bits of shrimp or fish scraps and get them to bite before they think. The strike of the snapper is fast and the hook must be set instantly, or the bait will be stripped clean from the hook. I have watched people feed them great numbers of ten cent shrimp before they got the hang of it. You almost need to anticipate the strike and set the hook before they bite!

My son and I have fished with Captain Paul Glanville of Islamorada who has several guaranteed honey holes for snapper. He says the mangrove snapper are always accommodating when sometimes the more glamorous species are not, or when the weather blows out other types of fishing. There are many smaller keys in the backcountry which are surrounded by shallow grass flats. If you pole up to the mangrove fringe you typically

*Myrna Leonard displays a nice mangrove snapper caught on a live pilchard and jig at Ninemile Bank.*
Courtesy of Hank Brown.

find deeper water where the tides rush around the tiny islands. These troughs may only be a little wider than the boat, but hold many fish in three feet of water.

Captain Glanville exclusively uses HOOKUP jigs baited with shrimp, and tosses them under the overhanging mangrove branches. Conditions are best when the water is moving and the current carries your bait next to the mangrove roots. Captain Glanville showed us how to get the rigs deep into the mangroves and horse out the keeper size snappers. We showed him several times how to get your line completely tangled in the branches of the trees. Sometimes I think the mangrove trees eat more jigs than the fish do.

Mangrove snapper are difficult to catch on artificials and are "leader shy" in clear water. They are frequently caught on artificial lures in cloudy water. Chumming in

*The HOOKUP jig and shrimp is a guaranteed "snapper-getter".*
Photo by Martin Smithson.

72

clear water does seem to reduce their shyness. Another proven method in clear water is to locate the fish during the day and begin fishing at dusk. Sunset and the hour or two following can be very productive. Just be prepared for nighttime navigation and the evening bugs.

Live baits, versus cut bait, account for the larger snapper in the Keys. There are several baits in the herring family that can be used. Whether it's actually a herring, sardine, menhaden, shad or pilchard, just ask for pilchards at the bait shop. They'll know what you mean. Or, if you're good with a cast net, you can collect them yourself.

Captain Hank Brown loves to fish with pilchards in the fall of the year. He will carry 200 to 300 baits in his live-well and head to the backcountry channels. For example, on the channels cutting through the Ninemile Bank, Brown will anchor and drift back over the channel. He uses some of the pilchards for chum and hooks one through the mouth on a jig. This method definitely attracts the larger fish.

Mangrove snapper are not the best fly fishing targets. However, some are occasionally taken off the trail of a muddying ray that has stirred up bottom dwelling creatures such as small crabs and shrimp. A shrimp-like fly pattern, similar to bonefish and permit flies, will sometimes fool a snapper under these conditions. The combination of throwing a fly into an area that has been chummed also increases the odds of hooking up on fly.

Mangrove snapper are delicious table fare and seem to be plentiful enough so that you don't feel guilty for keeping two or three fish. There is a five fish total and ten inch length limit. Be sure and check the current regulations before you go out.

# Personal Notes

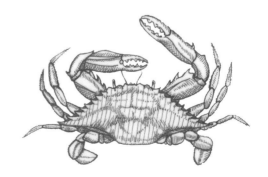

# Great Barracuda
## (*Sphyraena barracuda*)

Description: long, pike-shaped body, dull to bright silver sides with a greenish cast above; whitish belly; dark stripes on sides in varying numbers. Large jaw with jagged teeth, lower jaw protruding.

Similar fish: southern sennet

Where found: worldwide in warm waters, in bays and near bridges. Young live in inshore seagrass beds; adults range from inshore channels to open ocean. Range from Massachusetts to southeast Brazil.

Size: Average 5-10 lbs. in Florida Bay and larger to 50 lbs. near reefs. World record is over 100 lbs.

Remarks: Contrary to legend, barracuda do not attack waders or swimmers. Some bites have occurred when swimmers were wearing bright, flashy objects in turbid water. Small fish may be safe to eat, however, larger fish are sometimes very toxic.

The barracuda is usually considered a bonus catch because most are caught while looking for other fish. They provide great sport for the flats angler because they attack lures with a fierce crash. They give a high speed fight and can make spectacular head over tail jumps. They don't have the endurance of a bonefish but can generate an initial run like one.

Recently while poling around a flat and small island on the bayside, I was ready with a white bucktail jig tipped with a piece of shrimp. My son was poling and I was just casually looking for signs of fish and enjoying the scenery. Suddenly about 50 feet away there was a spray of small needlefish frantically trying to escape an unwelcome predator. I cast the jig and it was seized the very microsecond that it hit the water, followed by a high speed, but short run. My son yelped bonefish!! Then the fish leaped and turned a flip. The next yelp was barracuda! The three pound fish had caused some brief excitement and rejuvenated our interest that hot afternoon.

Barracuda will strike topwater plugs with such an explosion that your heart will either speed up or stop all together. On one occasion I was drifting the deep edge of the flat just west of Lignumvitae Key. It was late in the afternoon and everyone was worn out from fishing that morning so I went alone. I was throwing a topwater Heddon Zara Spook looking for some barracuda action. I tried reeling as fast as possible to stimulate some interest but got no takers. I finally lapsed into one of those late afternoon states of great mental abstraction. I stopped the plug about ten feet from the boat with my mind a million miles away when the bottom dropped out under the plug as a huge cuda made quick work of the mono leader and stole my $5 plug. After I regained my composure, I motored on home.

A lure that has become popular and is specialized for barracuda is the tube lure. A 12 inch piece of fluorescent colored surgical tubing is used which has a wire leader running through it. A treble hook is on one end with a second single hook in the middle and some leaded weight on the front end. Popular colors are chartreuse, yellow,

*The great barracuda will provide big gamefish excitement for any youngster.*
Courtesy of Papa Joe's Marina.

For the flyrod enthusiast, the barracuda may be one of the most overlooked gamefish. Cuda flies are tied with six to 10 inches of brightly colored synthetic material which can be braided, or just wrapped near the end, to look like a skinny needlefish. Similar flies use strands of fish-hair, another synthetic, where equal amounts of white, green and blue are overlaid and tied to a 1/0 or 2/0 hook.

A proven technique on fly is to cast in the vicinity of a cuda and immediately pick the fly back up off the water with a backcast. Repeat this cast and immediate backcast routine three or four times to thoroughly agitate the barracuda, then lay the fly down and strip quickly. A vicious strike will often follow. This technique is not restricted to sight casting only. There are many areas where blind casting on the flats or near channels will stir up some cuda action. Check the aerial photos where popular barracuda haunts are marked.

A word of caution regarding the handling of barracuda. They have very sharp teeth and love to leap, especially when near the boat. Be aware of their leaping ability and be prepared to fend off any accidental gashes. Use a towel or glove to hold the fish firmly while using pliers to remove the lure or fly. Revive the fish in the water like any other fish and release it when its strength is regained.

green and natural. The tube lure snakes through the water and gives the appearance of a needlefish, the cuda's favorite food.

Barracuda have keen eyesight and are exceptionally wary fish. Many times they will turn away after being spooked by a lure being cast too close. They may also refuse to strike after seeing you or the boat. The best approach is to cast as far from the boat as possible and a good distance away from the fish, maybe 50 feet. Raise the rod tip and retrieve the lure as quickly as possible in order to keep it skittering across the surface. If the cudas are interested they will streak in from great distances for the strike.

# Sharks
## Requiem Sharks: Family Carcharhinidae

*Sandbar shark.*

**Description:** This family includes the largest number of sharks, from small bottom dwellers to dangerous oceanic species. All have two dorsal fins, without spines. Most have broadly rounded heads. Common species found in the Keys and Florida Bay include the: bull, dusky, blacktip, spinner and lemon. They commonly reach six feet in length and are found in bays and estuaries to nearshore and offshore. The family's range is worldwide.

Long-time feared and avoided, sharks are gaining status as a big gamefish. There are over thirty varieties of sharks found off the Keys. Some guides are finding that sharks fill an important void when the weather conditions prevent fishing for some of the more glamorous species. When the winds have whipped up the bay waters, making sight fishing impossible, light tackle shark fishing is often a better option than not fishing at all.

When you consider a fish that averages three to six feet in length on the flats, is the world's most successful predator, is stronger than all its relatives, and is easily hooked on light tackle, why not? These animals instinctively seek deep water when disturbed, as a result of their deep oceanic ancestry. When hooked on the shallow flats that they occasionally investigate, they cannot dive deep, but bulldog out across the shallows. This can create some exciting battles.

Sharks respond primarily to scent. They have poor eyesight which makes it difficult to get them to take an artificial lure. They will, on occasion, bite a plug or fly if it is cast properly. The lure must be cast to the side of the shark and kept in the visible range of the side facing eyes. Even live bait, such as a big shrimp on a jig head, should be cast to the side where it can be retrieved past the eye in order to grab the shark's attention. Sharks can be unpredictable. Sometimes the motion attracts their interest. Other times they won't even look, completely ignoring your offering.

*Sharks are always willing to take your bait when other species turn finicky.*
Courtesy of Papa Joe's Marina.

77

The scent of fresh cut fish is definitely an attention-getter with sharks. The use of chum has been proven to stimulate sharks and excite them into taking an artificial. One technique for fly fishermen is to hang a dead, cut up, jack or barracuda over the side of the boat and drag it through the water. When sharks pick up the scent and begin to follow, you can cast right to them. Sometimes the carcass can be used as a large teaser. When the shark starts to home in on the teaser bait, it can be pulled away while a fly is cast in its place. The same can be done with a plug. The best flies are relatively large streamers with yellow and orange hackle. Mylar flash is added to make up for their poor eyesight.

An even more reliable technique, if you're just looking to get a shark on your rod, is to stake out or anchor and chum. Then place a hook into a chunk of the chum when sharks start to feed. Find the end of a long flat and position your boat near the deeper edge or just off the point of the flat. Sharks like to run the edges looking for opportunities to crash bait against the shallow banks. Once you've anchored, toss a half dozen pieces of jack or blue runner out from the boat. Repeat every 10 minutes. Be rigged with a chunk of bait on a 4/0 or 5/0 hook.

Regardless of what you use, fresh bait, plugs or flies, you will need a short length of coated wire leader. Monofilament is no match for shark teeth. It is also a good idea to use bronze hooks, even on fly, because it is unlikely you will risk getting slashed while removing a hook from a shark's mouth. The bronze hook will disintegrate quickly if you have to forfeit the fly or rig.

If you do outwit the prehistoric muscle and instinct of a shark, be careful when releasing the animal. Sharks have a skeleton made of flexible cartilage versus stiffer bones and can turn around and bite their own tail, or someone's hand grasping their tail. Extreme caution is in order. Use gloves, handle the animal quickly, and cut the line or leader if you cannot get the hook out easily with long nose pliers. Whatever you do, do not bring the shark into the boat. Keep the fish along side of the boat and release it alive. Do not gaff the fish. Remember, it is no longer macho to kill a shark.

In Florida Bay you may also encounter a large rusty brown shark, sluggishly cruising or lying motionless. These are nurse sharks which feed on bottom dwelling crustaceans and shellfish. They rarely strike anything you cast to them and do not put up much of a fight if they are hooked. They are best left alone.

# Florida Keys Fishing Calendar

## January/February

- Oceanside shorelines best for bonefish. Also downtide edges of flats where water is warmest.
- Good barracuda action on flats.
- Snook and small tarpon at bridges—evenings best.
- Deeper holes against mangroves good for mangrove snapper.

## March/April

- Backcountry heats up for trout, redfish and sharks.
- Oceanside bonefish begin to move up on flats.
- Tarpon start to move from bridges to flats.
- Permit action picks up.

## May/June

- Big tarpon begin to show at major Keys bridge channels.
- Sight fishing for the big tarpon on flats is best by June.
- Bonefish run shallow flats and tail often.
- Good months for permit and barracuda in shallows.
- Backcountry active for snook, redfish and trout.

## July/August

- Redfish and snook action still good in backcountry.
- Barracuda and sharks frequent the flats.
- Big tarpon may last through second week of July.
- Bonefish and permit best targeted in morning and evening.

## September/October

- Big bonefish on flats.
- Large mangrove snapper found in backcountry cuts.
- Shark, barracuda and permit on flats.
- Snook and tarpon follow bait run through bridges.

## November/December

- Same as October until water temperatures drop.
- Numerous tarpon in 30 lb. range.

79

Ever

Cape Sable

East
Cape

19

Flamingo

20

21

Snake
Bight

R:

22

Clive
Key

15

Pelican
Keys

16

• Sandy
Key

14

• Rabbit Key
Basin

Bar

Florida
Bay

N

↑

8

9

10

Long
Key

• Duck
Key

Marathon

• Vaca Key

• Boot Key

• Fat Deer
Key

80

# Aerial Photographs

Biscayne Bay

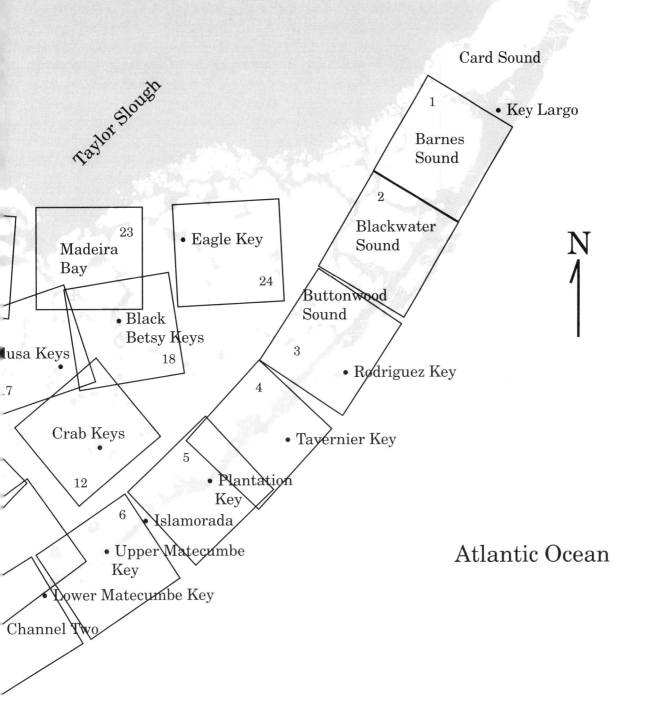

Card Sound

1

• Key Largo

Barnes
Sound

2

Blackwater
Sound

Taylor Slough

23

Madeira
Bay

• Eagle Key

24

Buttonwood
Sound

• Black
Betsy Keys

18

3

• Rodriguez Key

usa Keys

7

4

Crab Keys

• Tavernier Key

5

12

• Plantation
Key

6

• Islamorada

• Upper Matecumbe
Key

N

• Lower Matecumbe Key

Channel Two

Atlantic Ocean

*GIS data courtesy of Rayner Howard of Brevard Teaching and Research Labs, Palm Bay, FL.*
*Index map layout by Cape Canaveral Scientific, Inc., Melbourne Beach, FL.*

# *Personal Notes*

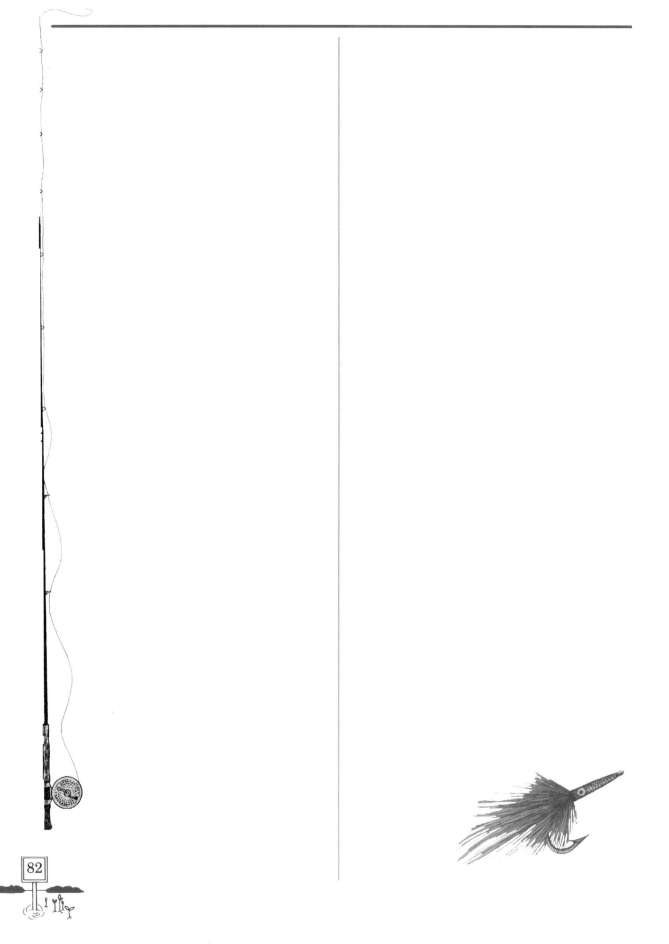

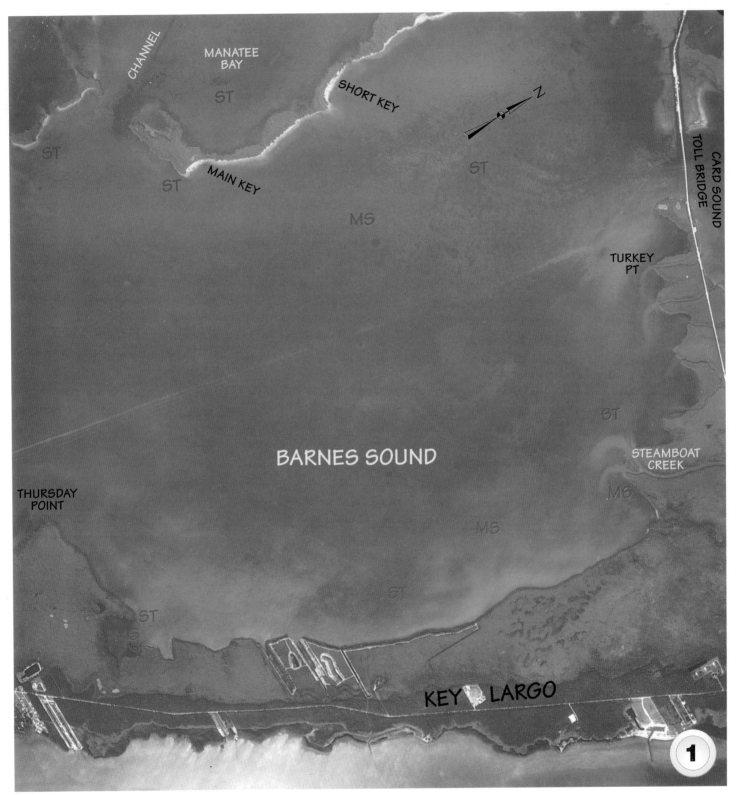

CHANNEL

MANATEE
BAY

ST

SHORT KEY

ST

ST

MAIN KEY

N

ST

MS

BARNES SOUND

THURSDAY
POINT

ST

ST

MS

ST

MS

KEY LARGO

CARD SOUND

TOLL BRIDGE

TURKEY
PT

ST

STEAMBOAT
CREEK

MS

1

**BN**=Bonefish
**BR**=Barracuda
**JK**=Jacks
**LD**=Ladyfish
**MS**=Mangrove Snapper

**PM**=Permit
**RD**=Redfish
**SK**=Snook
**ST**=Seatrout
**TP**=Tarpon

# Key Largo

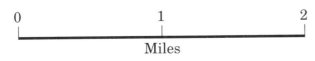

0          1          2

Miles

83

The Boggies

SK

MS

MARKED CHANNEL

MS
SK

ST

BLACKWATER PASS

RAMP

US HWY 1

MS

BLACKWATER SOUND

N

BUSH PT

ST

DUSENBURY CREEK

JEWFISH CREEK

SNAKE PT

LAKE SURPRISE

ST

US HWY 1

KEY LARGO

MS

ST

LARGO SOUND

MS

BN

BN

BN

BN

BN

PM

BN

BR

BN

2

# Key Largo

**BN**=Bonefish
**BR**=Barracuda
**JK**=Jacks
**LD**=Ladyfish
**MS**=Mangrove Snapper

**PM**=Permit
**RD**=Redfish
**SK**=Snook
**ST**=Seatrout
**TP**=Tarpon

84

0          1          2

Miles

WHALEBACK KEY

BN

RD

SHELL KEY

RD

MS

SWASH KEYS

ST

BUTTONWOOD SOUND

BAKER CUT

JK

MS

KEY LARGO

ST

DOVE KEY

SUNSET COVE

MS

BN

BN

RODRIGUEZ KEY

BN

BN

PM

LARGO SOUND ENTRANCE

BR

3

**Key Largo**

**BN**=Bonefish
**BR**=Barracuda
**JK**=Jacks
**LD**=Ladyfish
**MS**=Mangrove Snapper

**PM**=Permit
**RD**=Redfish
**SK**=Snook
**ST**=Seatrout
**TP**=Tarpon

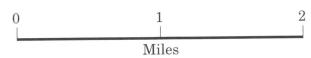

0       1       2

Miles

85

CROSS BANK

BN

ST

UPPERCROSS BANK

BN

PIGEON KEY

N

RAMSHORN SHOAL

ST

BN

COWPENS CUT

JK

HAMMER PT

BN

CREEK

HARBOR

KEY LARGO

TAVERNIER

BN

BN

PLANTATION KEY

BN

BN

BN

BR

TAVERNIER KEY

BN

4

# Tavernier

**BN**=Bonefish     **PM**=Permit
**BR**=Barracuda     **RD**=Redfish
**JK**=Jacks     **SK**=Snook
**LD**=Ladyfish     **ST**=Seatrout
**MS**=Mangrove Snapper     **TP**=Tarpon

86

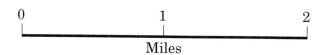

0        1        2

Miles

**Plantation Key**

BN=Bonefish
BR=Barracuda
JK=Jacks
LD=Ladyfish
MS=Mangrove Snapper

PM=Permit
RD=Redfish
SK=Snook
ST=Seatrout
TP=Tarpon

0       1       2

Miles

# Islamorada

**BN**=Bonefish
**BR**=Barracuda
**JK**=Jacks
**LD**=Ladyfish
**MS**=Mangrove Snapper

**PM**=Permit
**RD**=Redfish
**SK**=Snook
**ST**=Seatrout
**TP**=Tarpon

0          1          2

Miles

FIESTA KEY

BANKS

N

CHANNEL FIVE

CHANNEL TWO

TP
TP
TP
TP
TP
TP
TP
TP

BN
BN
BN
BN
BN

MATECUMBE BIGHT

LOWER MATECUMBE KEY

⑦

**BN**=Bonefish
**BR**=Barracuda
**JK**=Jacks
**LD**=Ladyfish
**MS**=Mangrove Snapper

**PM**=Permit
**RD**=Redfish
**SK**=Snook
**ST**=Seatrout
**TP**=Tarpon

# Lower Matecumbe
# Channels 2 & 5

0        1        2
Miles

89

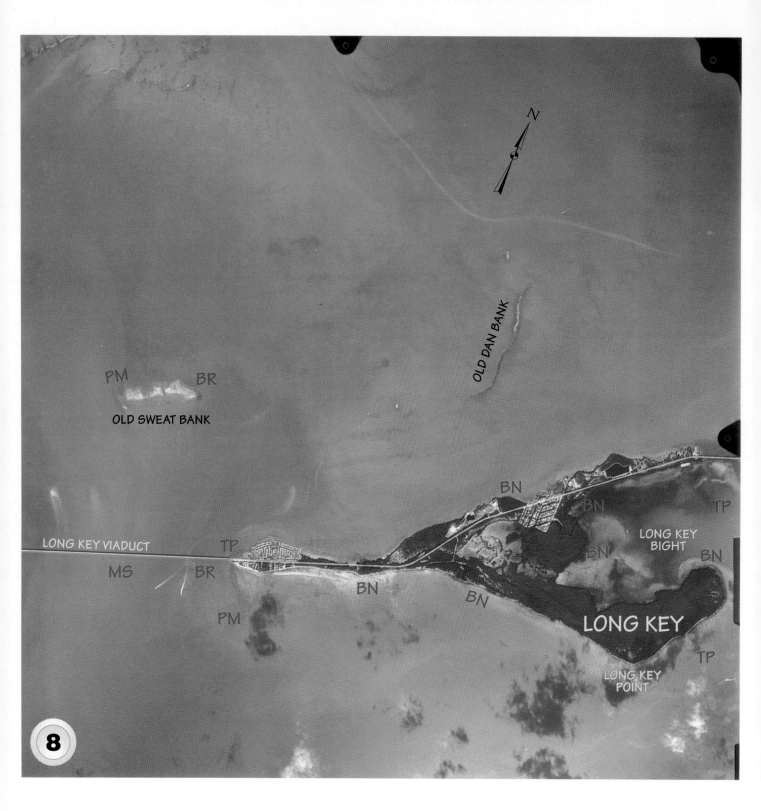

# Long Key

**BN**=Bonefish
**BR**=Barracuda
**JK**=Jacks
**LD**=Ladyfish
**MS**=Mangrove Snapper
**PM**=Permit
**RD**=Redfish
**SK**=Snook
**ST**=Seatrout
**TP**=Tarpon

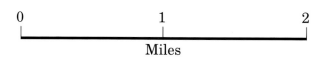

**Grassy Key**

BN=Bonefish    PM=Permit
BR=Barracuda    RD=Redfish
JK=Jacks    SK=Snook
LD=Ladyfish    ST=Seatrout
MS=Mangrove Snapper    TP=Tarpon

0      1      2

Miles

91

BR
MS

BAMBOO KEY

VACA KEY

MS

LONG
PT
KEY

FAT DEER
KEY

CRAWL
KEY

BN

GRASSY KEY

BN

DEER KEY

BN

**10**

# Grassy Key to Upper Marathon

**BN**=Bonefish
**BR**=Barracuda
**JK**=Jacks
**LD**=Ladyfish
**MS**=Mangrove Snapper

**PM**=Permit
**RD**=Redfish
**SK**=Snook
**ST**=Seatrout
**TP**=Tarpon

0              1              2

Miles

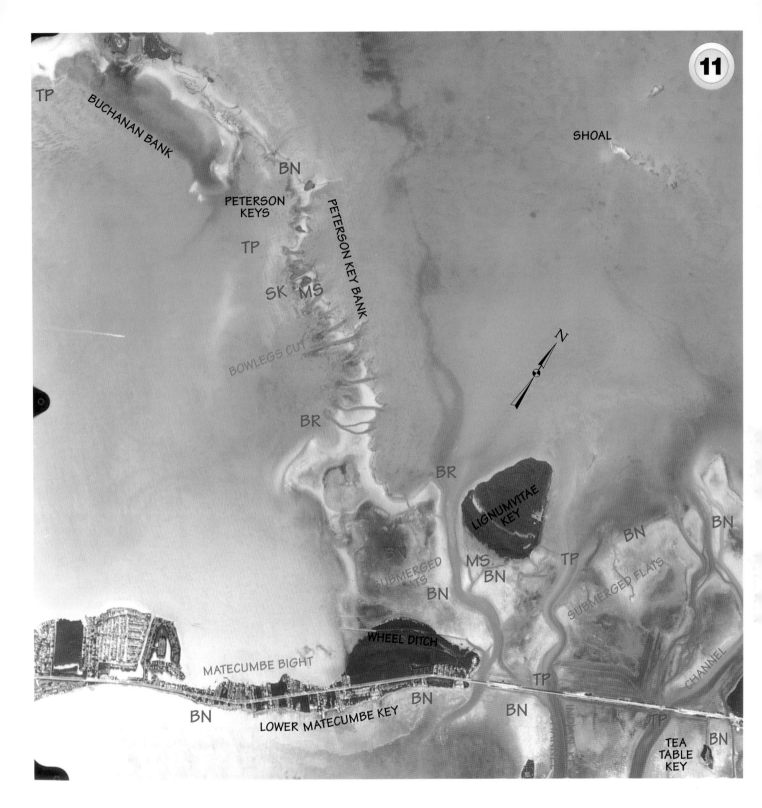

TP
BUCHANAN BANK
SHOAL
11
BN
PETERSON KEYS
PETERSON KEY BANK
TP
SK MS
BOWLEGS CUT
N
BR
BR
LIGNUMVITAE KEY
BN
SUBMERGED FLATS
MS BN
TP
BN
SUBMERGED FLATS
BN
WHEEL DITCH
CHANNEL
MATECUMBE BIGHT
BN
TP
BN
BN
TP
BN
LOWER MATECUMBE KEY
TEA TABLE KEY
BN

| | |
|---|---|
| **BN**=Bonefish | **PM**=Permit |
| **BR**=Barracuda | **RD**=Redfish |
| **JK**=Jacks | **SK**=Snook |
| **LD**=Ladyfish | **ST**=Seatrout |
| **MS**=Mangrove Snapper | **TP**=Tarpon |

# Florida Bay
# Islamorada

0          1          2

Miles

93

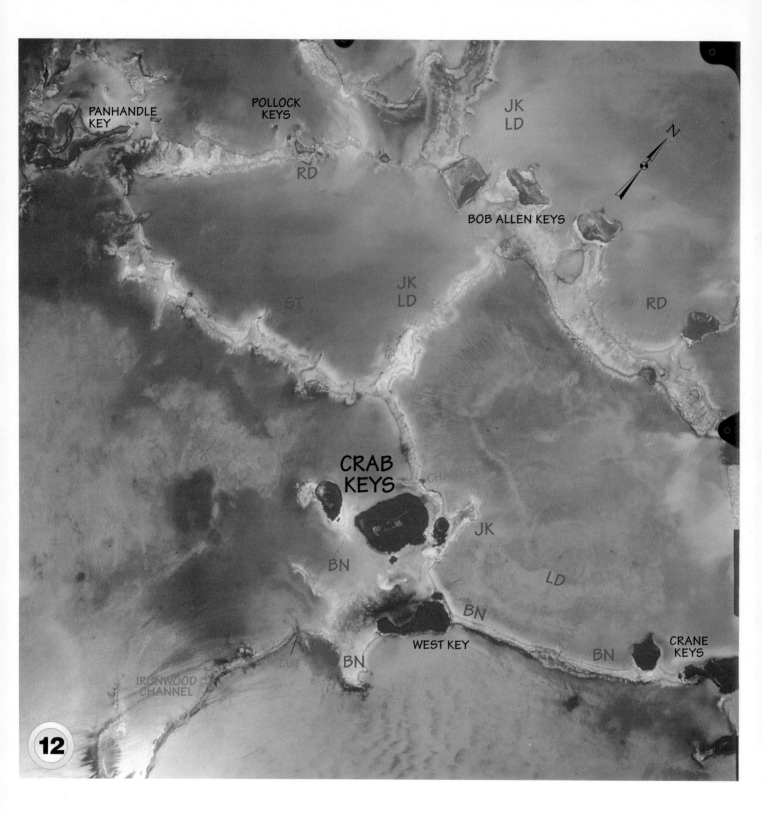

PANHANDLE KEY

POLLOCK KEYS

JK LD

RD

BOB ALLEN KEYS

ST

JK LD

RD

CRAB KEYS

CHANNEL

JK

LD

BN

BN

WEST KEY

BN

CUT

IRONWOOD CHANNEL

BN

CRANE KEYS

# Florida Bay
# Crab Keys

94

**BN**=Bonefish
**BR**=Barracuda
**JK**=Jacks
**LD**=Ladyfish
**MS**=Mangrove Snapper

**PM**=Permit
**RD**=Redfish
**SK**=Snook
**ST**=Seatrout
**TP**=Tarpon

0          1          2

Miles

12

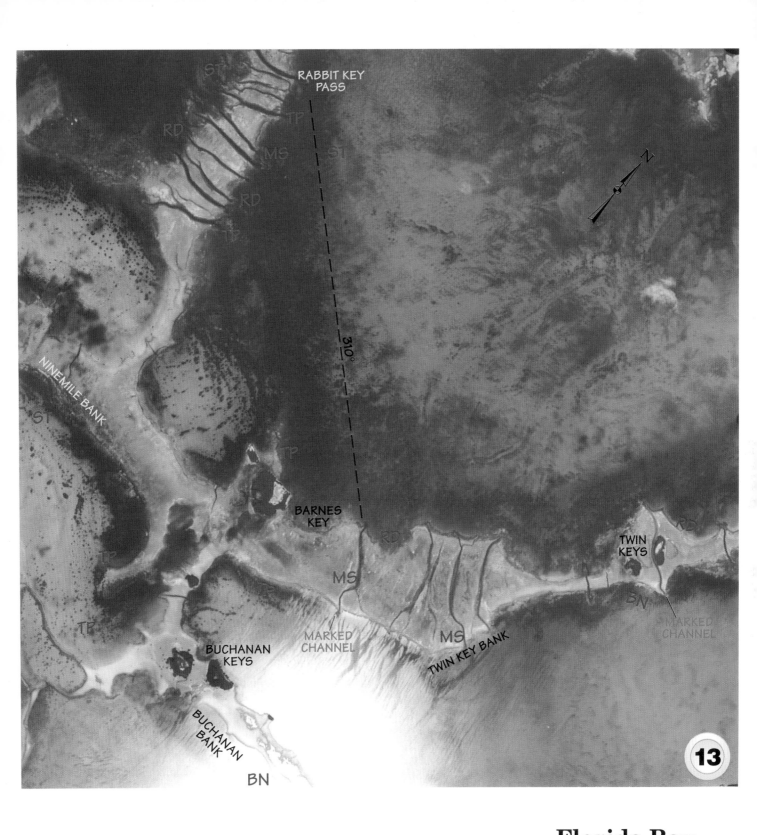

RABBIT KEY PASS

310°

NINEMILE BANK

BARNES KEY

TWIN KEYS

MARKED CHANNEL

MARKED CHANNEL

TWIN KEY BANK

BUCHANAN KEYS

BUCHANAN BANK

BN

**13**

BN=Bonefish
BR=Barracuda
JK=Jacks
LD=Ladyfish
MS=Mangrove Snapper

PM=Permit
RD=Redfish
SK=Snook
ST=Seatrout
TP=Tarpon

# Florida Bay
# Barnes Key

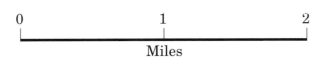

0          1          2

Miles

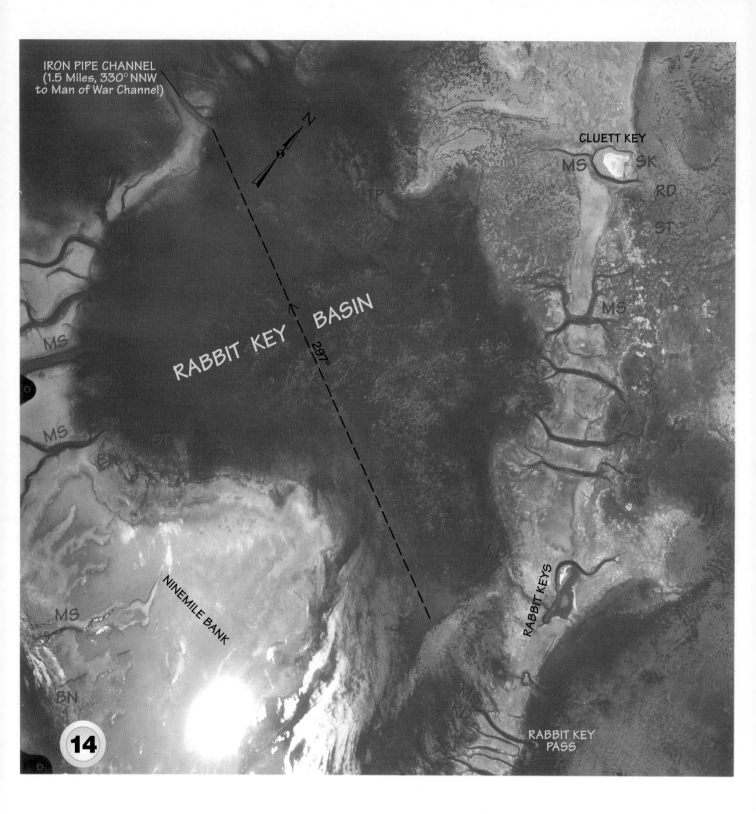

IRON PIPE CHANNEL
(1.5 Miles, 330° NNW
to Man of War Channel)

N

CLUETT KEY

MS    SK

RD

ST

TP

MS

RABBIT KEY BASIN

297°

MS

MS

ST

ST

BN

TP

MS

NINEMILE BANK

RABBIT KEYS

LD
RD

MS

BN

RABBIT KEY
PASS

**14**

# Florida Bay
# Rabbit Key Basin

| | |
|---|---|
| **BN**=Bonefish | **PM**=Permit |
| **BR**=Barracuda | **RD**=Redfish |
| **JK**=Jacks | **SK**=Snook |
| **LD**=Ladyfish | **ST**=Seatrout |
| **MS**=Mangrove Snapper | **TP**=Tarpon |

0        1        2

Miles

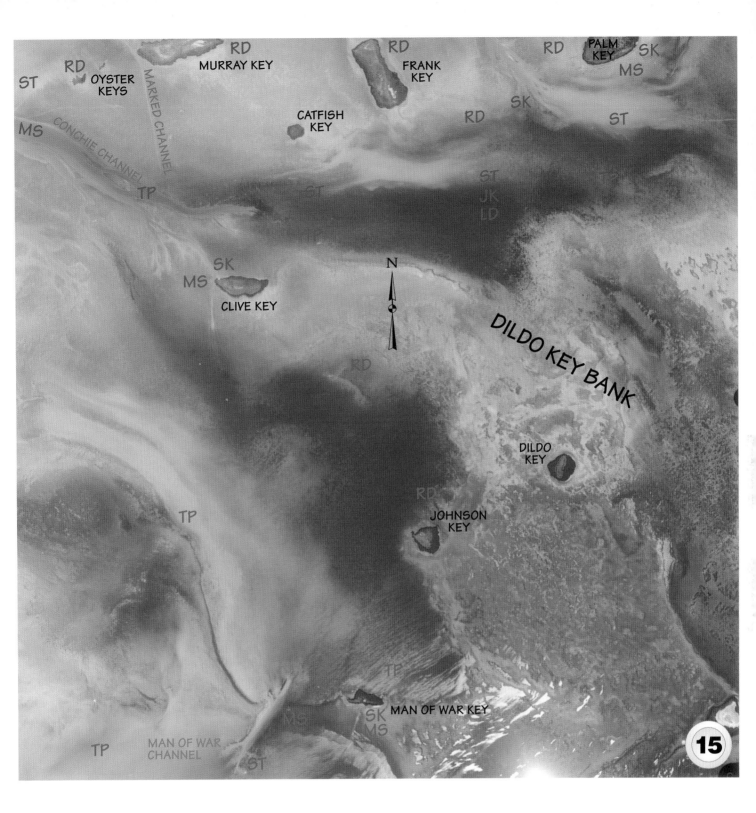

RD
ST
RD OYSTER KEYS
MS
MARKED CHANNEL
CONCHIE CHANNEL
TP
RD MURRAY KEY
CATFISH KEY
ST
RD FRANK KEY
RD
SK
ST
JK
LD
RD PALM KEY SK
MS
ST
SK
MS CLIVE KEY
N
RD
TP
RD
DILDO KEY BANK
DILDO KEY
JOHNSON KEY
TP
SK
MS
MAN OF WAR KEY
TP
MAN OF WAR CHANNEL
ST

**15**

BN=Bonefish
BR=Barracuda
JK=Jacks
LD=Ladyfish
MS=Mangrove Snapper

PM=Permit
RD=Redfish
SK=Snook
ST=Seatrout
TP=Tarpon

# Florida Bay
# Clive Key

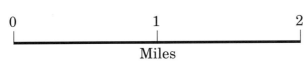

0          1          2

Miles

97

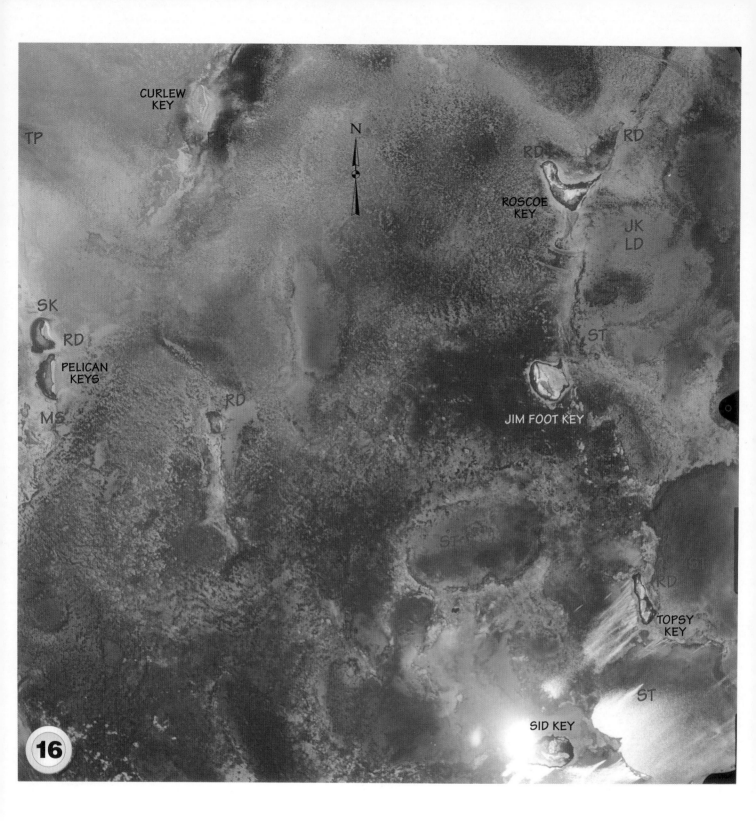

CURLEW
KEY

TP

N

RD
RD

ROSCOE
KEY

JK
LD

SK

RD

PELICAN
KEYS

MS

RD

ST

JIM FOOT KEY

ST

RD

TOPSY
KEY

ST

SID KEY

**16**

# Florida Bay
# Pelican Keys

98

**BN**=Bonefish
**BR**=Barracuda
**JK**=Jacks
**LD**=Ladyfish
**MS**=Mangrove Snapper

**PM**=Permit
**RD**=Redfish
**SK**=Snook
**ST**=Seatrout
**TP**=Tarpon

0          1          2

Miles

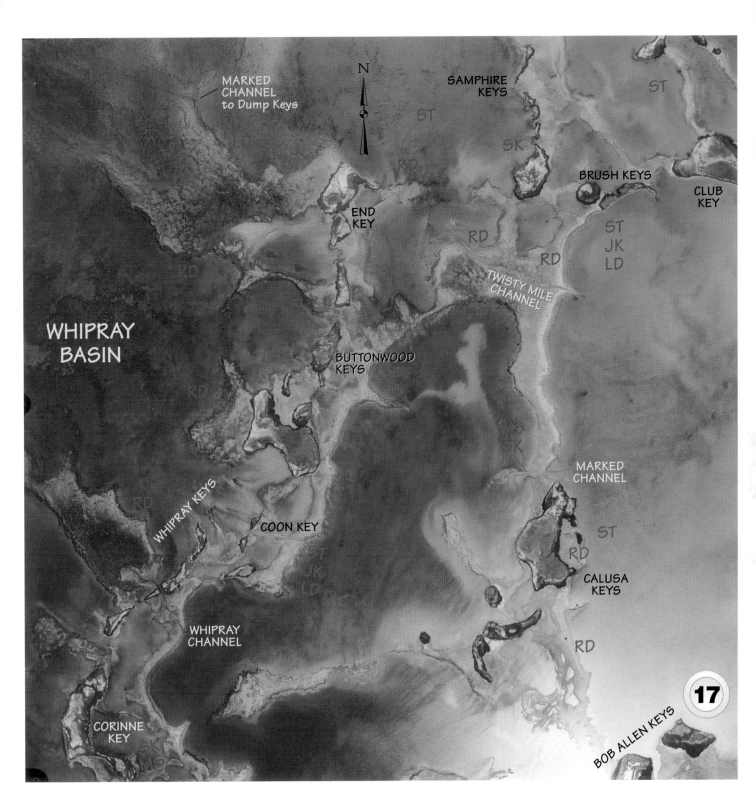

MARKED CHANNEL to Dump Keys

N

SAMPHIRE KEYS

ST

ST

SK

BRUSH KEYS

CLUB KEY

RD

END KEY

RD

ST JK LD

RD

RD

TWISTY MILE CHANNEL

WHIPRAY BASIN

BUTTONWOOD KEYS

RD

RD

SK

MARKED CHANNEL

WHIPRAY KEYS

COON KEY

ST JK LD

ST

RD

CALUSA KEYS

WHIPRAY CHANNEL

RD

CORINNE KEY

SK MS

17

BOB ALLEN KEYS

BN=Bonefish
BR=Barracuda
JK=Jacks
LD=Ladyfish
MS=Mangrove Snapper

PM=Permit
RD=Redfish
SK=Snook
ST=Seatrout
TP=Tarpon

# Florida Bay
# Calusa Keys

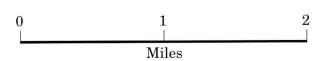

0      1      2

Miles

99

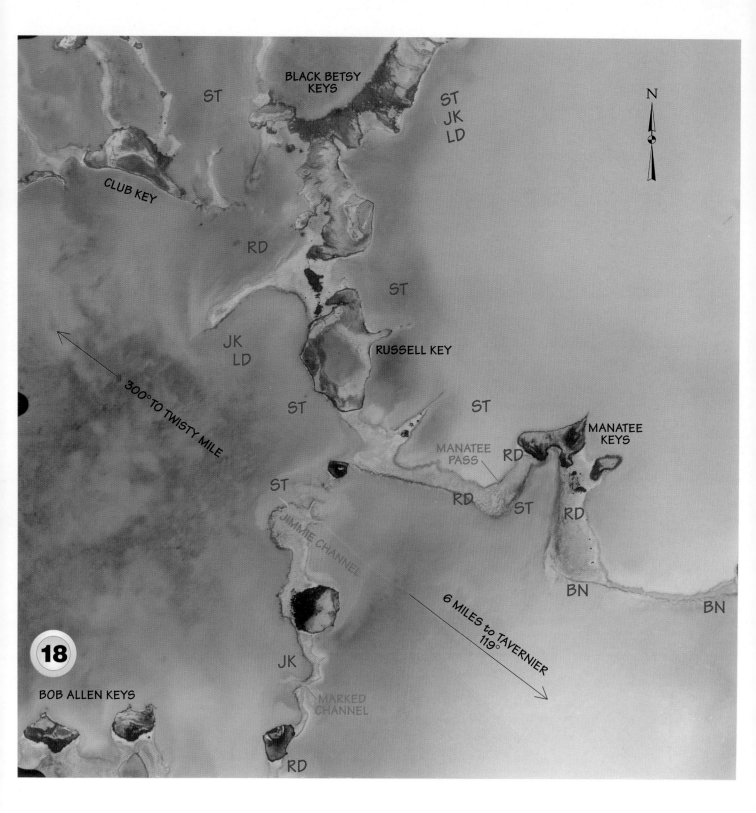

**BLACK BETSY KEYS**

ST

ST
JK
LD

N

CLUB KEY

RD

ST

300° TO TWISTY MILE

JK
LD

RUSSELL KEY

ST

ST

ST

MANATEE KEYS

MANATEE PASS

RD

ST

RD

RD

ST

RD

JIMMIE CHANNEL

6 MILES to TAVERNIER 119°

BN

BN

**18**

JK

BOB ALLEN KEYS

MARKED CHANNEL

RD

# Florida Bay
# Russell Key

**BN**=Bonefish
**BR**=Barracuda
**JK**=Jacks
**LD**=Ladyfish
**MS**=Mangrove Snapper

**PM**=Permit
**RD**=Redfish
**SK**=Snook
**ST**=Seatrout
**TP**=Tarpon

100

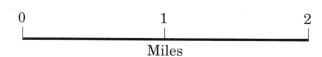

0          1          2

Miles

EVERGLADES NATIONAL PARK

N

CAPE SABLE

CANOE

LAKE INGRAHAM

CANOE TRAIL

ST

HIGH TIDE
ONLY

SK

RD

RD

SK
MS

HOUSE DITCH

EAST CAPE CANAL

TP

SK

TP

MS

EAST CAPE

TP

SK
MS

TP
SK
RD
ST

ST
RD

MIDDLE GROUND

**19**

**BN**=Bonefish
**BR**=Barracuda
**JK**=Jacks
**LD**=Ladyfish
**MS**=Mangrove Snapper

**PM**=Permit
**RD**=Redfish
**SK**=Snook
**ST**=Seatrout
**TP**=Tarpon

# East Cape
# (Cape Sable)

0          1          2

Miles

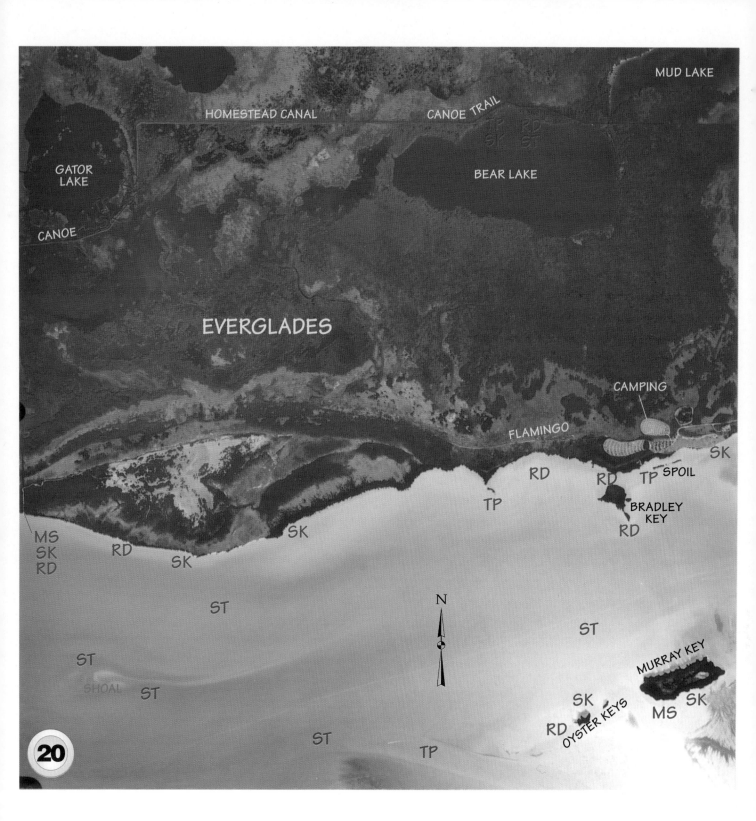

MUD LAKE

HOMESTEAD CANAL

CANOE TRAIL

TP
SK

RD
ST

GATOR LAKE

BEAR LAKE

CANOE

EVERGLADES

CAMPING

FLAMINGO

SK

RD

RD

TP SPOIL

TP

BRADLEY KEY

MS
SK
RD

RD

SK

RD

SK

ST

N

ST

ST

MURRAY KEY

ST

SHOAL

ST

SK

ST

RD

OYSTER KEYS

MS SK

TP

# Flamingo Area

**BN**=Bonefish
**BR**=Barracuda
**JK**=Jacks
**LD**=Ladyfish
**MS**=Mangrove Snapper

**PM**=Permit
**RD**=Redfish
**SK**=Snook
**ST**=Seatrout
**TP**=Tarpon

102

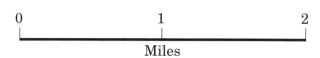

0          1          2

Miles

20

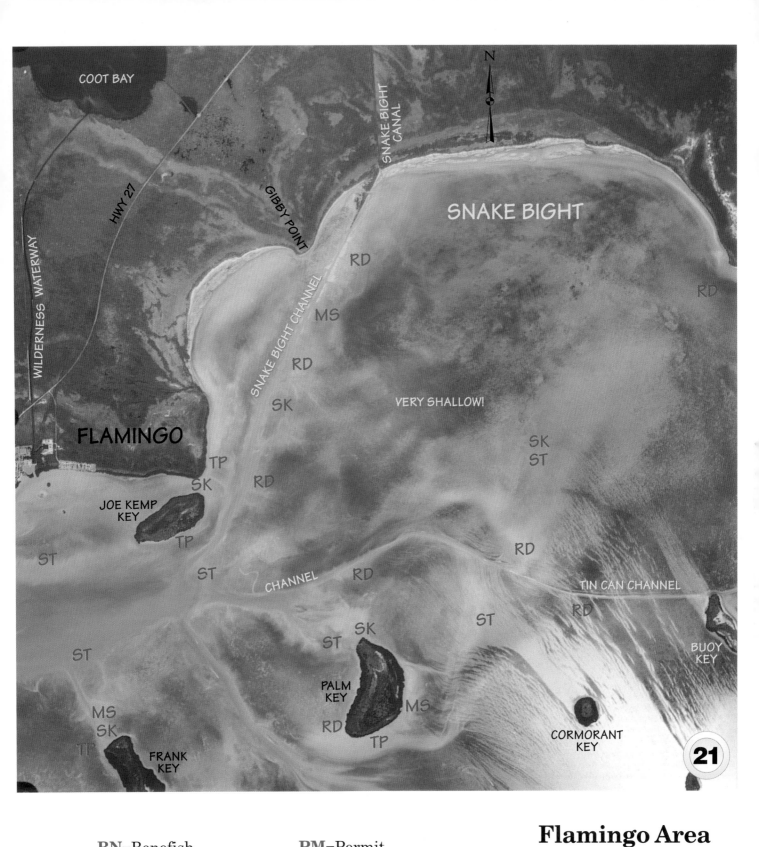

COOT BAY

N

SNAKE BIGHT CANAL

HWY 27

GIBBY POINT

SNAKE BIGHT

WILDERNESS WATERWAY

SNAKE BIGHT CHANNEL

RD

MS

RD

RD

SK

VERY SHALLOW!

SK
ST

FLAMINGO

TP

SK

JOE KEMP KEY

RD

RD

TP

ST

ST

CHANNEL

RD

TIN CAN CHANNEL

RD

ST

ST

ST

SK

RD

BUOY KEY

PALM KEY

ST

MS
SK

MS

CORMORANT KEY

TP

RD

FRANK KEY

TP

**21**

| | |
|---|---|
| **BN**=Bonefish | **PM**=Permit |
| **BR**=Barracuda | **RD**=Redfish |
| **JK**=Jacks | **SK**=Snook |
| **LD**=Ladyfish | **ST**=Seatrout |
| **MS**=Mangrove Snapper | **TP**=Tarpon |

# Flamingo Area

0          1          2

Miles

103

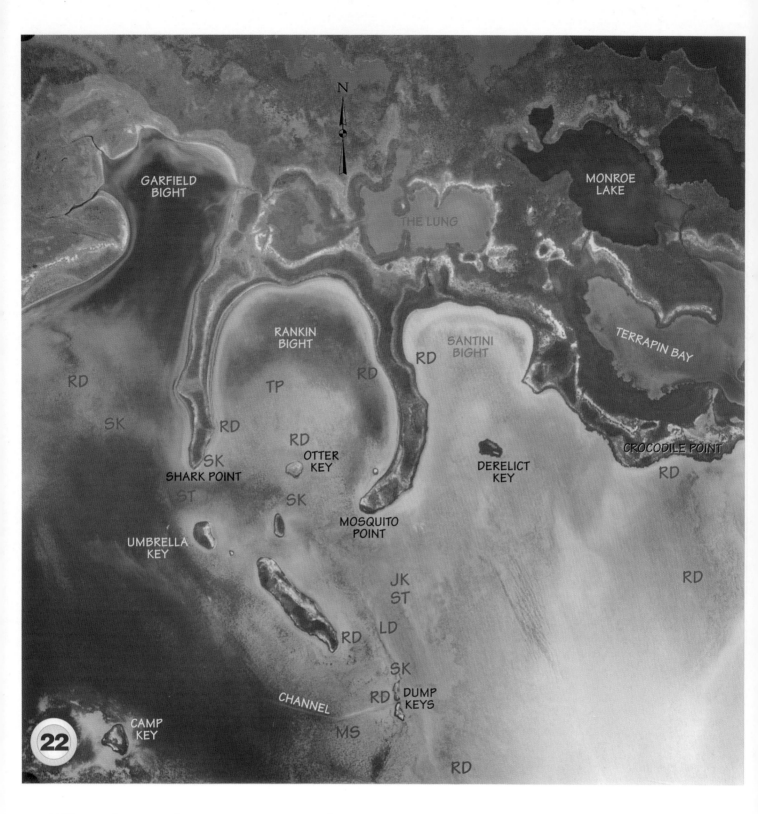

# Flamingo Area

**BN**=Bonefish
**BR**=Barracuda
**JK**=Jacks
**LD**=Ladyfish
**MS**=Mangrove Snapper

**PM**=Permit
**RD**=Redfish
**SK**=Snook
**ST**=Seatrout
**TP**=Tarpon

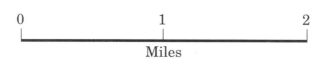

```
0                    1                    2
├────────────────────┼────────────────────┤
                   Miles
```

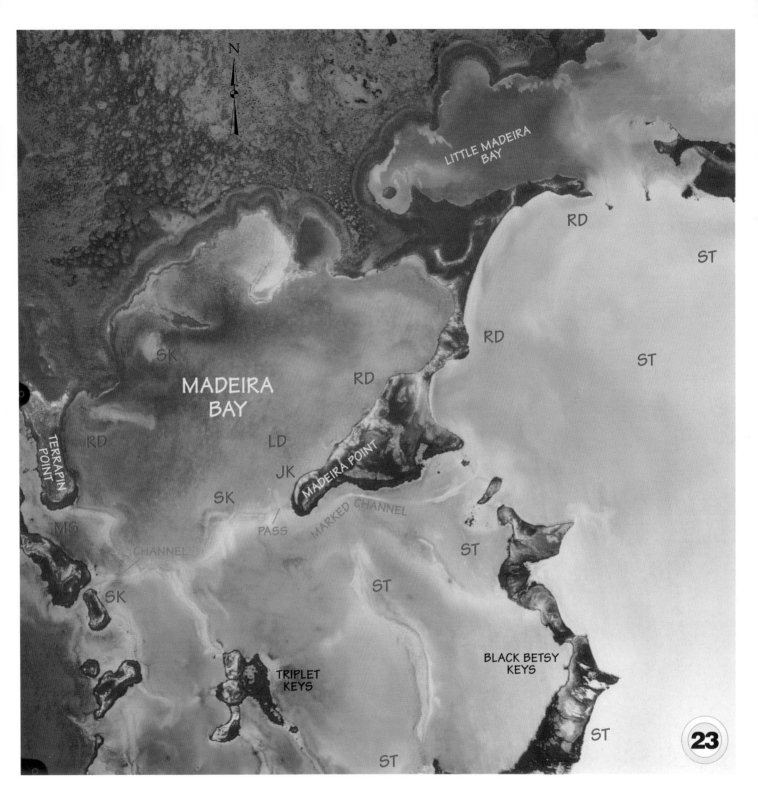

LITTLE MADEIRA BAY

RD

ST

ST

RD

RD

MADEIRA BAY

SK

RD

ST

LD

JK

MADEIRA POINT

SK

MARKED CHANNEL

TERRAPIN POINT

RD

MS

PASS

CHANNEL

ST

SK

ST

SK

BLACK BETSY KEYS

ST

TRIPLET KEYS

ST

ST

**23**

BN=Bonefish
BR=Barracuda
JK=Jacks
LD=Ladyfish
MS=Mangrove Snapper

PM=Permit
RD=Redfish
SK=Snook
ST=Seatrout
TP=Tarpon

# Northeast Florida Bay

0          1          2

Miles

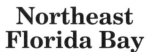

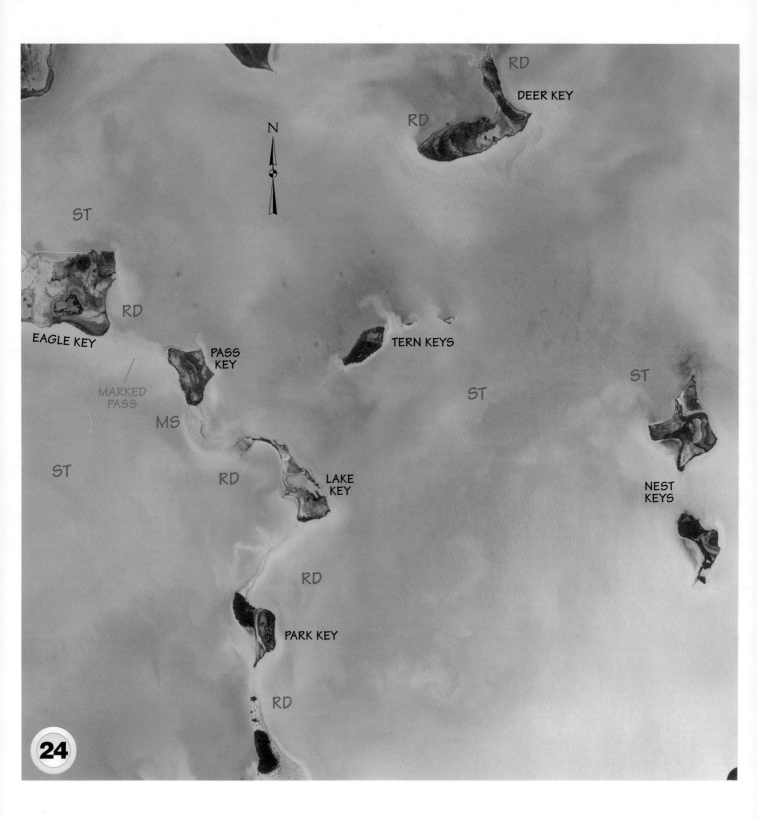

# Northeast
# Florida Bay

BN=Bonefish     PM=Permit
BR=Barracuda     RD=Redfish
JK=Jacks     SK=Snook
LD=Ladyfish     ST=Seatrout
MS=Mangrove Snapper     TP=Tarpon

106

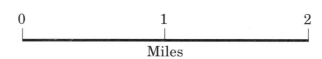

0             1             2

Miles